COULDN'T CARE MORE

A Study of Young Carers and Their Needs

COULDN'T CARE MORE

A Study of Young Carers and Their Needs

A report based on research which was commissioned and funded by:

Hampshire County Council Social Services Department and North and Mid Hampshire Health Commission

and managed by:

The Children's Society Community Development Team of Winchester Diocese.

Jenny Frank

The Children's Society
MAKING LIVES WORTH LIVING
A VOLUNTARY SOCIETY OF THE CHURCH OF ENGLAND
AND THE CHURCH IN WALES

Charity Registration No. 221124

Hampshire County Council

SOCIAL SERVICES DEPARTMENT

First published in 1995 by
The Children's Society
Edward Rudolf House
Margery Street
London WC1X 0JL
Tel. 0171-837 4299

A catalogue record for this book is available from the British Library.

ISBN 0 907324 96 7

Acknowledgements

I would like to thank everyone who has given their time to assist me during the course of this research. Their support and advice has enabled me to produce a detailed and representational report on the needs of young carers in Hampshire County Council Social Services Department, Winchester area.

Naturally, my deepest thanks go to the young carers themselves and to their families, who have welcomed me into their homes and allowed me to listen to their very personal experiences.

I hope this report will contribute to future professional practice and benefit young carers, their families and all those who work to support them.

Jenny Frank

Other acknowledgements

Hampshire County Council Social Services Department for their assistance with figures and tables.

Pauline Owen for section 7.4, The Winchester Young Carers Project, pages 67–68.

CONTENTS

FOREWORD

Although the issue of young carers is not new, it is only in recent years that their particular problems are beginning to be recognised. This piece of research undertaken in Hampshire County Council Social Services Department, Winchester area adds a new and important dimension to the small but growing body of literature on the issue. It is the first study to focus on young carers in a more rural setting, to highlight the role of an even more hidden group of children who are supportive carers and to record the views of older, former young carers.

Jenny Frank has three children and her second daughter has had cerebral palsy since birth so she has first-hand experience of the demands of caring and the effect that having a family member with a disability can have on family life. This has helped her to empathise with the constraints and feelings experienced by the young carers in this research.

The report indicates the importance of raising awareness among all professionals especially general practitioners and staff working in schools.

'All primary and senior schools were targeted first as this was the most likely means of contacting as many children as possible. Although a detailed letter was sent explaining the nature of the project and indicating possible signs which could point to a child being a young carer, no schools knew of any possible or confirmed young carers apart from one primary school, which sent notification at a later date. Most of the young carers were found through working closely with the adult social services teams and health care managers.'

The study shows that although many young carers are caring for someone with a physical disability, there was a significant number caring for a parent with mental health problems. It is important to note that although many children who care do cope well and gain a sense of achievement, they may experience some anxiety, stress or depression. We must therefore be aware of meeting their needs for practical support but not overlook their emotional needs. Among the conclusions that the report draws is the fact that:

'The care receivers are receiving services but the needs of young carers are not being directly addressed.'

In order to do this a multi-agency approach between adult and children's services is essential.

Hampshire Social Services, in particular those who work in the Winchester area and North and Mid Hampshire Health Commission are to be commended for their forward thinking approach in commissioning this research. The partnership with The Children's Society enabled the research to focus on many of the wider aspects of young carers. The strengths of the recommendations lie in their multi-agency approach, which will harness the commitment of all major providers of resources to children and adults.

Jenny Frank's work gives a clear and comprehensive view of young carers, their families and the way professional services respond to the different situations. Her checklist and guidelines will be valuable to anyone working with families where children are caring. I hope this will subsequently mean more recognition and support for the young carers.

I am delighted to see the culmination of this research which will provide a valuable resource to anyone interested in what is a current and sensitive issue. Jenny Frank is to be congratulated for her dedication and hard work in producing this report.

SYLVIA HEAL
National Young Carers Officer
Carers National Association

PREFACE

This study of young carers in Hampshire County Council Social Services Department, Winchester area was commissioned by Winchester Children and Families Planning and Liaison Group. It was funded by Hampshire County Council Social Services Department and North and Mid Hampshire Health Commission. Initially the period of research was to be six months but it soon became evident that the depth of work needed in order to do justice to the needs of young carers required a longer timescale. The total period of research was therefore extended to eight months, with a further period allocated for discussion and editing.

The aim of the research was to provide information on numbers of young carers in the Winchester Social Services Area, identify their major needs, present guidelines to advise services on the future development of professional practice and to suggest a model for the ongoing monitoring of young carers' needs.

This piece of research is the first to be conducted in an area which has such a large rural population. However, although the findings are specific to HCCSSD, Winchester area, the issues faced by families and young carers in this area mirror those found in other research projects which were based in more urban areas and inner cities.

The Children's Society is committed to raising public awareness about issues affecting children and young people and to promoting the welfare and rights of children and young people in matters of public policy. The management of this project by their Community Development Team of Winchester Diocese gave the project an independent status, which in turn provided flexibility to work with all agencies and facilitated contact with families and children.

The information contained in this report was obtained by talking to the young carers, their families, and appropriate professional and voluntary agencies. It was also supported by relevant background reading. The young people who were interviewed came from a range of family backgrounds but all had one factor in common: caring responsibilities for a parent or sibling suffering from a long-term illness or disability. The words and experiences of the young people have been compiled to provide an insight into their needs in order to advise service providers on the future development of professional practice. Some of the young people's words make painful reading and serve to underline the sensitive nature of undertaking any research or supportive work in this field.

The impact of caring on these children's lives should not be underestimated; it is only the degree that varies. Not only do young carers live with the day to day issues and anxieties associated with the illness or disability of someone close to them, but they also have their own childhood and development restricted by the demands of caring.

Although many young carers may cope well and gain a sense of achievement or self-worth from their responsibilities, the effect of caring on their lives can be dramatic. However, it does not necessarily follow that all of these families and young people are in crisis. Rather, they are asking to be heard, believed and, where appropriate, to be given relevant support.

The level of obligation and strain which caring may impose on the carer makes them a legitimate object of concern for Welfare Agencies.

S. BILSBORROW, *YOU GROW UP FAST AS WELL: YOUNG CARERS ON MERSEYSIDE*, BARNARDOS, 1992

In recent years social welfare policy has highlighted the key role that all carers have to play in supporting families where there is an illness or disability. There is a growing awareness that they are a valuable resource to community care.

A young carer is a child or teenager under the age of 18 who has responsibility for the care of a parent or family member who is suffering from a long-term illness or disability. The caring role may be physical, emotional or both.

In this study the following criteria were used to define a young carer.

A child under the age of 18 where a member of the family has:

- a physical or learning disability;
- a long-term limiting illness;
- problems concerning mental health;
- alcohol or drug abuse related problems;

which has resulted in that young person being placed in a caring role. The following categories of young carer were identified:

- children who are the sole carer in the home;
- children who are supporting another adult family member in care tasks for the care receiver (care receivers include not only parents of the child but also grandparents and siblings who have an illness or disability);
- children of the above families who were also taking on parenting responsibilities for younger brothers and sisters because their parents were unable to or needed assistance at specific times.

1.1 Aims and purpose of the study

The project was funded and commissioned in order to:

- investigate the needs of young carers in the area of research;
- ascertain the extent of their need for support;
- present guidelines which will advise services on the future development of professional practice;
- suggest a model for the ongoing monitoring of young carers' needs.

1.2 The area of research

Winchester

The City of Winchester is noted as a religious and educational centre. It is home not only to a famous cathedral, but also to Winchester College, the oldest major public school in England. Nevertheless, it has a mixed economy and a population representative of any similar sized city in the south of England.

Although Winchester is not generally thought of as a city that has substantial needs, most statistics in fact correlate with the national average. The mixture of social classes and needs are 'hidden' by the traditional image of the city. In some cases, such as incidence of mental health problems, needs are actually higher than the national average. There has also been a rise in the number of older, heavily dependent members of the population, which has increased pressure on care management services. In addition, the transient population of travellers present their own pattern of demand on services. There is a projected rise in the number of children under 3-years-old and a growing percentage of children are known to the local authority as 'in need'.

Unlike larger major cities, Winchester does not have a strong infrastructure of high profile support services or voluntary groups. The neighbouring and much larger city of Southampton is relied upon to provide many facilities such as hospice care and refuges.

54 percent of the total population live in a rural area and this affects accessibility to information and services. In simple, practical terms it takes a care manager or keyworker much longer to visit clients in outlying rural areas than those living within the centre of Winchester. Equally, clients in rural areas are less able to attend clinics, day centres or support groups which are based in the city than clients who live within easy reach.

The population of surrounding villages has undergone a change over the last decade. Villages now mainly provide housing for commuters and the rural farming communities of earlier years have diminished. This has an effect on the community as many new residents do not assimilate into the villages, which leads to fragmentation of community and neighbourly support.

The network of support that does still exist is intrinsic to each village and is not linked to any central services. Hampshire Council of Community Service are currently setting up a network of village representatives to act as co-ordinators of information. In many areas residential housing has outgrown local services resulting in inadequate recreational and community facilities. Many villages have sparse public transport services, which compounds difficulties faced by families who have a member who is ill or disabled.

The specific area covered by this study is Hampshire County Council Social Services Department, Winchester area (see Figure 1.1). It differs very slightly from the Winchester City Council Area, which also includes Boarhunt, Southwick and Denmead. It is a large area geographically, which has a population with diverse needs. With the recent move to care in the community, it provides a challenge, which might continue to increase as more people who may previously have gone into residential care choose to remain in their own homes.

Table 1.1 below shows total population figures for Winchester City Council Area and HCCSSD, Winchester area. It also shows the total number of residents considered to be of 'parentable ages' (ie. aged 16–19), and the total number of household residents with a long-term limiting illness or disability in the Winchester area.

Table 1.1 Population statistics

	1991	1995 (projected)
1. Total residential population of Winchester City Council, of which 54% is rural.	98,067	100,882
2. Total residential population of HCCSSD, Winchester area.	90,828	93,300
Total household residents aged 16–59 (assumed parentable age)	51,030	
Household residents with a long-term limiting illness or disability		
aged under 16	271	
aged 16–44	1,109	
aged 44–59	1,260	
aged 60–74	2,845	
aged 75 or over	2,772	
Total	8,257	

(All population figures have been taken from the 1991 OPCS.)

The total population of Hampshire is 1,595,014. To assist comparison with other regions, Appendix 5 contains a range of tables which show Hampshire's population placed within a national context. Appendix 4 shows the number of household residents with a long-term limiting illness in Hampshire.

Also of note is the data in Appendix 5 which shows the low number of people from ethnic minority groups, and the fact that 22.4 percent of the people in Hampshire recorded as 'sleeping rough' were in the Winchester area.

Although the findings of this research are specific to the Winchester area, they also correlate with findings of research conducted by projects based in denser urban areas. This report underlines the fact that, wherever they live, the needs and emotions of young carers are universal.

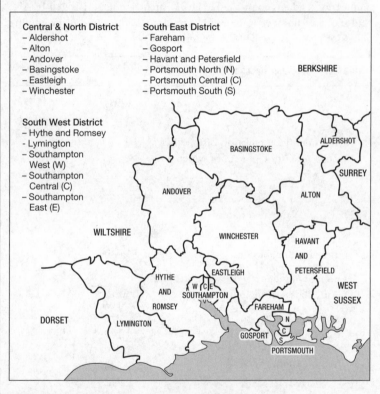

Central & North District
– Aldershot
– Alton
– Andover
– Basingstoke
– Eastleigh
– Winchester

South East District
– Fareham
– Gosport
– Havant and Petersfield
– Portsmouth North (N)
– Portsmouth Central (C)
– Portsmouth South (S)

South West District
– Hythe and Romsey
- Lymington
– Southampton West (W)
– Southampton Central (C)
– Southampton East (E)

Figure 1.1 Hampshire County Council Social Services Areas 1994

1.3 Numbers of young carers found

Table 1.2 on page 5 shows the number of children and young people who were known to be caring, or strongly believed to be doing so. Of this total, 74 were confirmed young carers and 17 were unconfirmed but were included because the family structure or circumstances strongly point to the child caring as there is no one else able to do so.

Table 1.2 Number of young carers identified

Number of children and young people found to be:

caring for parents	78
caring for a grandparent	2
caring for siblings with disabilities	11
Total	91

Of these, the eldest was 17-years-old and the youngest 3-years-old.

Figure 1.2 below shows age, gender and location of the young carers. As it was difficult to obtain full details of the 17 unconfirmed young carers, some of the information below is recorded as unknown.

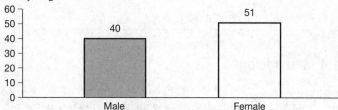

(i) Numbers of young carers identified according to gender

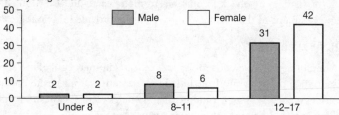

(ii) Numbers of young carers identified according to age and gender

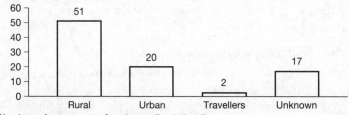

(iii) Numbers of young carers found according to location

Figure 1.2 Young carers identified according to gender, age and location

Table 1.3 below shows the illnesses and disabilities of the care receivers in the homes where young carers were identified.

Table 1.3 Illnesses and disabilities of care receivers

Alcohol related illness	5
Arthritis	2
Congenital paralysis	3
Drugs related illness	2
Heart/stroke condition	3
Mental health problems	18
Multiple Sclerosis	21
Road accident injury	4
Visual impairment	2
*Other	10

*(including ME, hearing impairment and rare degenerative complaints)

1.4 Methodology

The following section looks at the difficulties involved in identifying the young carers and making contact with their families. It outlines the structure of the interviews and describes the sensitivity required in conducting them and the need to respect the privacy and confidentiality of the families involved. Limitations to the research are also detailed with an assessment of the accuracy of the statistics provided on young carers.

Reference group

A multi-agency reference group was set up and met regularly to support and guide the research. It included representatives from health and social services (both adults, and children and families teams), education welfare, The carers development advisor (Hampshire County Council Social Services Department) and The Children's Society Community Development Team of Winchester Diocese.

Liaison with the Carers National Association also gave direction and provided valuable advice.

Identification of young carers

As found by other researchers in this field, primary identification of young carers was a very time-consuming task.

Contacts were made initially with appropriate statutory organisations including schools, health and social services, and voluntary groups, with a two fold aim:

- to establish the level of awareness of young carers and their needs amongst professional and voluntary groups;
- to gather information on possible young carers.

All primary and senior schools were targeted first as this was the most likely means of contacting as many children as possible. Although a detailed letter was sent explaining the nature of the project and indicating possible signs which could point to a child being a young carer, no schools knew of any possible or confirmed young carers, apart from one primary school, which sent notification at a later date. Most of the young carers identified were found through working closely with the adult social services teams and health care managers.

During the initial contacts, concerns about ethical issues and the confidentiality of clients were expressed. A commonly held view was that the children and families may not have been willing to participate or that it might have been detrimental to the stability of the family or the welfare of the care receiver if they were to be involved in the project. Similar views were also found by Sandra Bilsborrow in her study *You Grow Up Fast As Well: Young Carers on Merseyside.*

Obtaining the names and details of children who were known or strongly believed to be caring took many weeks. Case workers often had to refer to their line manager before releasing any details. Reassurance that the aim of this project was not to criticise past lack of recognition was needed in some cases. It proved particularly difficult to gain any detailed information about families where the care receiver had a mental health, drug or alcohol related illness. This is discussed in more detail on pages 22–23.

The data requested were initially collected on a standard form (see Figure 1.3 on page 8). All informants were assured that the details were for research reference only, would not be shown to anyone else or published in that format. Despite this reassurance, which was strictly adhered to, some were still unhappy, or unable (due to insufficient knowledge about the family) to provide the required information, so in some cases details were sparse. This reluctance or inability to provide details was particularly pronounced when a child's parents had alcohol or drug related problems, or were travellers.

Figure 1.4 on page 8 shows the percentage of referrals which were provided by the statutory and voluntary agencies contacted and Table 1.4 shows a breakdown of all targeted contacts and their responses.

Young Carers – Winchester Area

Please indicate the number of young carers under 18 years known to you. Also record any past young carers who are now aged between 19 and 25. Please complete your own details at bottom of page. Thank you.

	Initials of young carer	Year of birth	Male or Female	Nature of illness/ disability of care receiver	Sole Carer or Supportive
eg	K.F	1980	M	Agrophobia	Supportive
1)					
2)					
3)					
4)					

Name _____

Department or organisation _____

Contact address _____

_____ tel _____

Figure 1.3 Sample form circulated to statutory and voluntary organisations

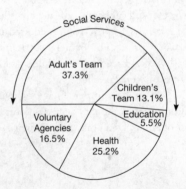

Figure 1.4 Percentage of referrals from statutory and voluntary agencies

Table 1.4 Numbers of young carers referred to the project by targeted agencies

Social services

Care Attendant Scheme	16
Adult Mental Health and Physical Disabilities Team	11
Adult Learning Disabilities Team	6
Specialist Social Workers for Hearing Impaired and Visually Impaired	★
Children and Families Team	12
Royal Hampshire County Hospital Social Work Department	1
Total	46

Health

Manager for the Young Physically Disabled	16
School nurses	1
School doctors	0
General practitioners	0
Winchester Specialist Community Health Team	7
Health visitors and community nurses	1
Total	25

Education

Education Welfare and the Advisor to Travellers	4
Schools	1
Total	5

Other contacts

Voluntary groups	13
Other young carers	2
Alcohol Advisory Service	0
Drug Advisory Service	0
Youth Service	0
Child Guidance Service	0
Community Police Service	0
Total	15

(★ These service providers did know young carers but the families were outside the research area.)

It is interesting to note that some services which did not respond or gave a nil return had in fact been in contact at some time with a young carer recorded in the research but were possibly unaware of the child's role.

The following did not provide direct contact but were invaluable for swift dissemination of information: HantsNet, Information Exchange and Winchester and District Council of Community Service. More details about these can be found in Appendix 1.

Once the initial list of identified families where it was either known or strongly believed that a child was caring was obtained, further meetings were then held with informants to discuss which families could be approached and to gather more details about each family if possible. All the families except two were known to service providers and most of the care receivers were already receiving some support in the home.

Interview sample

For a fully representational sample it might have been more appropriate to select children according to the category of illness or disability of the care receiver, but this was not possible. The sample is random in that only those families who volunteered were interviewed. Observations made by service providers were also used to gather information. However, it is very apparent from the quotes occurring throughout this report that the young carers have many needs in common, no matter who they care for.

Interviews

The process of contacting families was again very slow and time consuming. It took time to establish contact with a family and to arrange a mutually convenient time to visit. Once a family agreed to participate, the initial contact was made by phone in order to explain the nature of the project and stress that the visit would be informal and that if, on arrival, the child changed his or her mind then the interview would not take place. For some families, particularly those where the young carer was younger, more than one visit was arranged. Six of the families who participated lived in a rural area and consequently travelling time (sometimes as much as 30 minutes) increased the time required for each visit. The amount of time needed to travel to homes in rural areas significantly cut down the hours available to visit families. This factor is obviously common to anyone working in a rural area.

Most interviews were conducted in the family home and with the young carer alone. Two interviews were held at school and one interview could only be held in the presence of the care receiver.

Each interview lasted between one to two hours and a tape recorder was used to record the conversations. (Only one child declined the use of this.) The meetings were very informal, the aim being to direct questions and conversations in a way which would facilitate discussion of the same broad issues with each young carer. However, each meeting took into account the child's age and the interviewer's assessment of his/her social or emotional development, and was adapted accordingly. Opportunity was also given for the children to voice any issues which were important to them.

The interviews were based on determining for whom the young carer was caring, how and when they started to care, the type of tasks they undertook and how they felt about caring. When talking to younger children, a variety of stimuli were used, including colouring sheets and a visual aid of a cut away picture of a home with stick and peel figures and furniture. The most successful aid in encouraging the children to talk in a relaxed way was the game *All about Me* produced by Barnardos. It contains cards with the opening phrases of sentences such as:

I feel so angry about... The best dream I ever had... The worst thing about school holidays is... The best time of day for me is... I get embarrassed when... One thing I hate doing is... I wish I could tell dad this...

The cards were selected prior to the interview and during the interview turns were taken to pick a card and finish the sentence. This game was used with children aged from 8–15 years with equal success across the age range.

During the interviews it was necessary to gain the child's trust but at the same time not to raise any expectations which could not be fulfilled. Because some of the children were talking for the first time about their experiences and anxieties it was very difficult to be empathetic but avoid adopting the role of counsellor. It was also important not to appear judgemental or shocked by some of the children's words. Similar experiences are recorded by Sandra Bilsborrow in *You Grow Up Fast As Well: Young Carers on Merseyside*. This is an important point which needs to be noted before talking to young carers for the first time. Dealing with issues raised by the young carers is described on page 12, under 'Ethical issues and confidentiality'.

Table 1.5 Details of those who participated in interviews

1 sole carer over 12-years-old
9 supportive carers over 11-years-old (1 of these was the main carer)
3 supportive carers under 11-years-old
3 sibling carers over 11-years-old

Total number of young carers interviewed   16

Also spoken to during the course of the research were two former young carers under 25, both still caring now; two former carers over 25, no longer caring; three parents who took part in detailed interviews and three parents who gave shorter interviews. In addition, a range of service providers and managers both in the statutory and voluntary sector provided relevant information throughout the research.

Former young carers

Throughout the period of research, it became increasingly clear that the effects of caring as a child have a lasting impact and remain with a person throughout adult life. Adults ranging in age from 22 to mid 50s were encountered who had cared for a parent or sibling when they were a child.

The research criteria limited the investigation to former young carers up to the age of 25, so people above this age were not actively targeted. However, several came forward of their own accord and recounted their memories and feelings. Approaches were often made by former young carers following an open meeting or discussion group on the research. They acknowledged that the issues and needs which had just been described were indeed part of their own childhood experience but that they had never previously thought of themselves as carers nor confronted the impact it had had on their lives.

Ethical issues and confidentiality

Informants were very concerned about their clients' confidentiality and so were assured that the interviews would be conducted in confidence and that care would be taken to ensure that any quotes used would remain anonymous. All the families who took part saw the report as a constructive means of achieving future support for themselves and their children. Only one care receiver declined to take part and she was not receiving any services into the home, nor was she in direct contact with any service provider. Although the child was known to education welfare services, they did not know the child was caring.

Conducting the interviews purely for research purposes was a difficult task. It was not easy to walk away from some children who had just expressed their innermost feelings. For many of them, it was the first opportunity they had had to express their needs and anxieties and in some cases, resentment and anger. Therefore, if it was felt that the child or family situation required immediate support then, with the agreement of the child and family, contact was made with the family's keyworker or the relevant service agency to try and effect appropriate help. This ranged from provision of counselling to arranging extra time for homework tasks to be completed. Contact was maintained with most of the families, either directly or through a keyworker, throughout the research period and all were thanked at the end of the project.

Analysis of findings

The recordings of the young carers' words were transcribed after the interviews. Outlines of discussions with keyworkers and parents, which were not recorded, were also written up immediately after any appointments. Recurring points and issues were expressed by the young carers, their parents and keyworkers and these are illustrated by the quotes which occur throughout the following chapters. Findings were also compared with other contemporary research work. Any similarities found regarding issues raised, needs of the children and perspectives of statutory and voluntary services were noted. Throughout the project the structure of the research and issues arising from it were discussed, in general terms, with the members of the reference group.

Quotes

Quotes are used extensively to document the evidence gathered in this report because they convey the situations and emotions of young carers and their families so clearly. The ages of the young carers are provided for some quotes but since protecting the confidentiality of the young carers and their families interviewed for the research was a priority, this was not always appropriate.

Limitations to the research

All except two of the families included in the statistics in this report were already known to service providers, although not all were receiving services. Further families who were unknown to services but may have a child who is a young carer were not discovered. In addition, even though the research period was extended there was not enough time to pursue busy or disinterested agencies who may have been aware of other young carers.

The statistics should therefore be viewed as partially representative of the true situation and possibly only showing the 'tip of the iceberg'. This is borne out by the fact that since the research period ended and awareness of the work carried out has continued to spread, more children who are young carers but were previously unknown to services have been identified. Thirteen more have since been drawn to the researcher's attention or have initiated contact themselves, but are not included in the statistics.

It proved very difficult to obtain details of families where the care receiver has an alcohol or drug related illness, or to establish the exact nature of the family situation. This also applied to families where the care receiver had a mental health problem. It was not possible to make contact with any of these families or their children and any information relating to them in this report was obtained through close contact with the family's keyworker or service provider. These details are discussed more fully on pages 22–23.

Because of the population profile in Winchester, the particular needs of ethnic minorities could not be studied. However, children of travellers are included.

Follow-up work

Because so many of the young carers expressed a need to be heard and to meet each other, a one-day pottery workshop for those over 12-years-old was arranged at the end of the research period. The young carers were collected from their homes and spent an afternoon painting and making pots, whilst getting to know each other. There was no emphasis placed on talking about their feelings or needs. The group has continued to meet even though the research phase of the project is completed and participants are helping to compile a local information leaflet. The most recent visit was to Fairthorne Manor, the YMCA National Outdoor Education and Training Centre, where the young people had an opportunity to try their hand at canoeing, abseiling and raft building.

1.5 Contemporary projects and resources

There are no official statistics which can be used to estimate the number of young carers in England and Wales but estimates based on three projects funded by the Mersey Regional Health Authority suggest that as many as 40,000 children could be young carers.

Much contemporary research has been conducted during the last few years, some of which is listed in the bibliography on pages 83–84.

The Carers National Association has a dedicated resource team for young carers and have produced a package of information for older, sole young carers. Information for project workers is also available, including further information on the Carers Bill (see page 15). Details can be found in Appendix 1.

Nationally, there are a growing number of projects offering support to young carers and their families, which have been established in different regional locations. A full list is available from the Carers National Association. In order to give an overview of the type of work being conducted nationwide, projects in different areas are briefly outlined below.

● Barnardos North West Division has established three projects under the Action for Young Carers plan in Liverpool, Wigan and Leigh, and Rochdale. The aims of the projects are to raise awareness regarding young carers and the issues affecting them, to direct services to young carers and their families and to work directly with young carers providing support that is relevant to their needs.

● Barnardos also manages a pilot support project in Leeds. This was established as a result of research by mental health practitioners in the area, which looked at the needs of children who have a parent with a mental health problem.

● Gloucestershire have a county development worker who is promoting awareness amongst agencies across the county and assisting in the development of appropriate services and support for young carers. Nine young carers groups are now established which are linked with youth and community centres, schools or social services.

● A project in Nottingham, managed by Crossroads, works alongside other agencies and provides support to individual young carers and groups.

● The Children's Society Neighbourhood Development Team is conducting a research project which aims to identify young carers in the Bath and Wansdyke area, and talk to them about their caring roles and support needs. Recommendations based on young carers' experiences and participation will then be made later on this year for future provision.

● Throughout the County of Hampshire, there have been several recent initiatives launched. A support group meets once a month in the family centre at Gosport, providing a resource for young carers in that district. Andover Health Trust recently organised a young carers week to raise public awareness of the need to recognise and support these children. Basingstoke has also started a support group and Southampton is in the early stages of considering young carers' issues.

1.6 Legislation and young carers

Young carers have always existed. They are not a new phenomenon but recent legislation and the move to care in the community have heightened awareness of their existence and of the duty that local authorities have to consider their needs when providing services.

The Carers (Recognition and Services) Bill

As this research was nearing completion, The Carers Bill received its third reading in the House of Lords and was then sent for Royal Assent. This bill was originally drafted by the Carers National Association and defines a carer as someone who provides a substantial amount of care to someone on a regular basis. It includes provision for young carers under the age of 18.

When enacted on April 1st 1996, it will place a duty on local authorities to carry out a separate assessment of the ability of a carer to provide and continue to provide care. If this assessment reveals that considerable burdens are being carried by the young carer, the local authority may be obliged to increase the level of service provision to the person needing care under the NHS & Community Care Act. In addition, local authorities should provide services direct to the young person if the effect of caring responsibilities are such that the child is deemed to be 'a child in need' under the terms of the Children Act.

The implications on funding to resource services to meet the requirements of the bill are already being discussed. The recommendations at the end of this report respond not only to this research but also to the requirements of the pieces of legislation referred to above. The relevant sections of the NHS & Community Care Act, the Children Act and other supporting legislation can be found in Appendix 2.

1.7 Local policy guidelines

Each local authority is required to produce policy guidelines which inform and advise their service providers.

The guidelines which are currently applicable to the needs of young carers or contain policy statements which can be used to allocate resources within HCCSSD, Winchester area are:

● Community Care Plan 1994/5 (Hampshire County Council Social Services Department)

● Think Carer (Hampshire County Council 1992)

● Children First (Hampshire County Council Social Services Department 1993) – A policy strategy for services for children and families

● Hampshire County Council – The Children Act – Policies and Procedures 1991

● Hampshire County Council Policy Statement on Children with Special Needs, 1995

Fuller explanatory notes on these policy documents can be found in Appendix 3.

Helping her is just part of life... I don't really remember it being any different. YOUNG CARER AGED 14

The young people who were interviewed came from a range of family backgrounds but all had one factor in common: caring responsibilities for a parent or sibling suffering from a long-term illness or disability. Six young carers lived in the city and the remaining ten lived in rural parts of the area.

In this chapter, the terms used to classify young carers throughout this report are defined and the question of how to determine acceptable levels of care is discussed. Particular issues and circumstances which affect young carers, including the dysfunctional effect caring can have on the family, false maturity, transfer of role and cross-gender caring are described. Specific reference to children of parents with mental health problems, or drug or alcohol related problems are also included. The last section looks at some of the reasons which cause children to become young carers.

2.1 Classification of young carers

In order to clarify the different caring roles adopted by the children, this section explains the criteria used to classify the young carers.

Sole carers

A sole or primary young carer is a young person or child who has sole responsibility in the home for care tasks needed by the care receiver because there is no other able adult in the home. In this study, the majority of children found to be sole carers have parents with a mental health problem, which includes illnesses such as agrophobia, schizophrenia and chronic depression. Tasks performed by them include housework, shopping, parenting younger siblings and taking responsibility for the parent's safety and medication on days when they are unable to do so themselves. Two families are included in which the young daughters, one aged 3 and another aged 4, perform household tasks and are responsible for their own self-care on bad days. One of these also reminds her mother to take her medication and assists with the administering of it. Three children were also found to be sole carers for both parents who were ill.

Supportive carers

Supportive young carers are children or young people who give assistance to an able adult who is the main carer in the home. This study particularly highlights the needs of children who are supporting an able adult carer within their family. Awareness that these children were caring was often veiled by the fact that there was already an able adult in the home who was presumed to be undertaking and coping with all the caring tasks. The majority of service providers assumed that if young carers did exist, they would be found in one-parent families. This study also discovered that in eight of the two-parent families, the children are in fact the main carer rather than the able adult. In all of these eight families, the care receiver is the mother. The partner is either involved in demanding full-time employment or shiftwork or simply does not see it as their duty to undertake the caring responsibilities.

The range of caring responsibilities undertaken by this group of young carers are as varied and, in some cases, as demanding as those carried out by sole carers. Additionally, one issue which was expressed by several children was the concern and feeling of responsibility they had towards the able, caring parent. The children were anxious because they often felt the able parent was doing too much, was under stress, unable to take a break and had no one to talk to. They felt that the responsibility of ensuring that the strain of caring was reduced lay with themselves.

My dad does everything and he gets very tired. He needs a break in the evenings. YOUNG CARER AGED 16

Some adult carers admitted that they could not cope if the child was not there. They were aware that possibly too much was asked of the child but there seemed to be no other solution.

Sibling carers

My brother is always awake early... and so when my father is away, I have to get up to help my mother sort him out. YOUNG CARER AGED 17

Recent research by NCH–Action for Children (Atkinson, N., Crawforth, M., *All in the Family: Siblings and Disability,* 1995) noted that 'over 98% of the 360,000 children with disabilities in the UK live with their families at home'. The NCH research studied the whole spectrum of needs of able siblings who have a brother or sister with a disability and found that the 29 children in the survey all helped to care for their brother or sister and were experiencing many stresses similar to those of their parents.

There is increasing recognition of those who have caring

responsibilities for their sibling. They too may require support as many of
their needs duplicate those of young carers who care for an adult relative.

This study identified eleven sibling carers and three of these were
interviewed. The three interviewed echoed the findings of NCH in that
they expressed a desire to escape the pressures at home at times and to
have the opportunity to spend more time with their friends.

On several occasions that I witnessed, the child [young carer]
wished to go out with friends. Her mother denied this request.
OBSERVER

I didn't really want to go on holiday with my parents this year but I
had to because they couldn't cope without me. YOUNG CARER

All the sibling carers had strong feelings of affection for their disabled
sibling and would not wish to be without them for a long period of time.

I feel really sad when my sister goes away for respite. YOUNG CARER
AGED 12

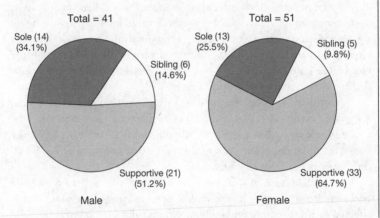

Total = 41

Sole (14)
(34.1%)

Sibling (6)
(14.6%)

Supportive (21)
(51.2%)

Male

Total = 51

Sole (13)
(25.5%)

Sibling (5)
(9.8%)

Supportive (33)
(64.7%)

Female

Figure 2.1 Numbers of young carers identified according to role and gender

In total 27 sole carers were identified, 53 supportive carers and 11 sibling
carers. It is interesting to note that 16 of the sole carers were caring for a
parent with a mental health problem and that all 11 sibling carers were
living in rural areas.

2.2 Acceptable levels of care

Helping out can be a healthy part of family life. But where this
becomes a responsibility there can be serious effects on a child's
personal and educational development. CARERS NATIONAL ASSOCIATION

Although many young carers cope well and gain a sense of achievement, self-worth or pride from their responsibilities, the effect of caring on their lives can be dramatic.

It is important to remember that children who care do so because a parent or other close family member is ill or has a disability. This fact alone can be the cause of associated emotional states such as anxiety, stress or depression in the child.

I get pain in my tummy when I think too much about mum.
YOUNG CARER

Caring can impose an added strain upon the child but in some cases it can also help them cope with the situation. To be prevented from caring when the child has a strong wish to do so could cause them to feel unwanted or isolated.

Assessing levels of care

When assessing a young carer's needs, consideration will need to be given as to whether the level of caring responsibilities that the child is undertaking are of an acceptable or unacceptable level. There can be no set guidelines for making this differentiation as each family's circumstances will vary and the impact of caring responsibilities on the child will also depend on their age, physical ability, emotional development, temperament and so on.

Ascertaining whether the child's caring responsibilities are of an acceptable or unacceptable level will be a dilemma faced repeatedly by anyone working with young carers. A child's wish to care for a loved one may need to be respected and sometimes the best course of action for all the family may be not to intervene.

The level of care provided by the child or young person may be considered unacceptable if the child's own welfare or development is affected or if it becomes physically or emotionally demanding.

It is difficult to know how much we do because she has MS or if we would be doing it anyway. YOUNG CARER AGED 16

There comes a point where you just want to leave and you think you can't take anymore. YOUNG CARER

2.3 Issues affecting young carers

False maturity

The majority of the young carers appeared to be responsible and mature beyond their years and expressed an adult attitude towards their situation and caring responsibilities. This false maturity was evident across the age range. For some it was a mask, which disappeared when given the opportunity, within the support group and elsewhere, to switch off from home life and its associated responsibilities. Some children also showed what could be described as a backlash to the false maturity, retreating into immature behaviour within the support group, where they felt able to relax. Others retained their 'adult' composure even when away from home. All young carers were competent in self-care skills.

Transfer of role

If there is a change of role by one member within a family, this is usually balanced by a compensatory change of role by another family member. One transfer of role that was observed amongst the young carers was that of an elder child taking over the parenting role for younger siblings when the able parent or care receiver were unable to do so. Such a change of role would appear to be an attempt by the young carer to maintain family stability.

In four of the families, the elder child would often look after younger able children at certain times of the day in order to assist a parent. In two families the elder child was very protective towards the younger able child, at times speaking for them. The younger child in turn looked to the older child for support.

Young carers who undertake responsibilities not usually associated with childhood are making a change to their customary role within the family in order to adapt to the situation. Developing the adult responsibility necessary to perform many caring tasks, which results in false maturity, is also another compensatory change of role which young carers undergo.

Such changes of role could affect a child's natural development and continue to affect them in later life. (See pages 53–54.)

Dysfunction

In some families this transfer of role had led to a dysfunctional relationship between young carer and care receiver, particularly in situations where there was a loss of parental authority as a direct result of the child's caring role. In some instances where the relationship between parent and child had become dysfunctional, the children said that the illness had never been openly discussed within the family and both parent (care receiver) and child avoided referring to the caring tasks, even when performing them. The children appeared to be supressing their own emotions, although strong feelings of anger towards their ill parent were openly expressed to the researcher.

Cross-gender issues

This study found a higher percentage of mothers receiving care than fathers. It also found that more sons had caring responsibilities for mothers, including personal care and toileting, than daughters for fathers. A total of 16 sons were found to be caring for their mothers (43 mothers were found whose children had caring responsibilities towards them) and a total of three daughters were found to be caring for their fathers (16 fathers were found whose daughters had caring responsibilities towards them). Two reasons why sons were caring for their mothers were that some of the mothers were either separated from their partners or their partners did not regard it as their role to perform caring tasks. Some of the care receivers acknowledged that this was not an ideal situation but either could see no obvious alternative or did not want an 'outsider' to perform these tasks. In the families where daughters were giving personal care to their fathers, this was mainly in a supportive role where it required two people to lift a man onto the toilet or into the bath or shower. Some daughters also took on sole responsibility for caring for their father at times in order to give their mothers a break.

Mental health problems

The research found 19 children caring for a parent with a mental health problem or under mental stress. 16 of these were sole carers. The youngest children to be found, two girls aged 3, were caring for a parent with a mental health illness. Identifying and supporting anyone who suffers from mental health problems can be a slow and difficult process so it should be expected that finding and approaching the children who care for them will prove an equally difficult and sensitive area of work in the future. The nature of the caring role is also less obvious than where there is a more 'visible' illness or disability within a family group.

It was not possible to talk to any families where the care receiver had a mental health problem. Although keyworkers would have liked families to be interviewed because they were concerned about the situation, they anticipated that the request would be rejected. Concern was also expressed that raising the issue of a child caring might not only be detrimental to the care receiver's health but could affect the fragile stability of the family. This poses the question of how to balance the needs of the care receiver, the young carer and the whole family without neglecting one or aggravating the other.

Information about children caring for parents with mental health problems was sparse but it was discovered that many were acting as parent to younger siblings when their ill parent was unable to cope. Some were ensuring their own parent's safety and reminding them when to take medication. Emotionally these children have to cope with any unpredictable behaviour patterns displayed by their parent, which could range from violent outbursts to silent withdrawal. A study in Leeds of former young carers of parents with mental health problems, conducted by Alison Elliot, gives an insight into the issues faced by this particular group of young carers and the emotional impact it has on them. (*Hidden Children: A Study of Ex Young Carers of Parents with Mental Health Problems in Leeds,* Leeds City Council Department of Social Services, 1992).

Drug or alcohol related illnesses

The research found five children with a parent suffering from an alcohol related illness or problem and three with a parent with a drug related problem. It is interesting to note that none of these referrals came from the drug or alcohol advisory units. David Stafford, director of St Joseph's Centre for Addiction, Haslemere, Surrey points out that 'only about 5% of all problem drinkers are treated directly or openly' and when treated it is 'the clients drinking that becomes the focus of attention. It is highly unusual for the whole family to be assessed for the effects on them of the drinking behaviour. Thus, the problems of the spouse and children are not taken into account and remain hidden.' (*Children of Alcoholics,* Piatkus, 1992).

Young carers in this group appear to be mainly undertaking household chores, preparing family meals and are often responsible for their own self-care. They also ensure their own parent's safety, in some instances guiding the parent home when incapable. The older children are also parenting their younger siblings on occasions when the parent is incapable. They too have to cope with unpredictable behaviour patterns in their parent. One former young carer whose parent had an alcohol problem was interviewed for this research. Some of her experiences are detailed in Chapter 5, pages 53–54.

It was not possible to talk to any of the families in this group either. It was thought that to ask the parent to consider if their own child was caring for them would be a very sensitive matter and require them to openly acknowledge that they had a problem. Keyworkers also felt that the parent may fear the possibility of their child being removed from them if there was any hint at inadequacy in parenting skills on their part and that this could cause them to withdraw from services completely.

Details gathered about children caring in both groups outlined above were verified by service providers in direct contact with the families.

Financial issues

Financial restraints were experienced by many families as, regardless of family income, having someone ill or disabled required a higher expenditure, which either came out of regular income or family savings.

Some families interviewed were unaware of the full range of benefits available. One family didn't feel they should claim for benefits and in two families the only source of income was from benefits. Young carers under the age of 16 are not eligible for benefits. Those who are over 16 may be eligible for Invalid Care Allowance if they are studying for less than 21 hours a week and the person being cared for meets the criteria as set down by the Department of Social Security (see Appendix 1).

2.4 Why do children become carers?

There was a strong impression that, whatever the provision of other help, children's assistance was a significant part of family existence. R. GRIMSHAW, *CHILDREN OF PARENTS WITH PARKINSON'S DISEASE*, NATIONAL CHILDREN'S BUREAU, 1991

General

In most families, the extra responsibilities associated with having a member of the family who is ill or disabled have developed gradually. As an illness progressed or the disabled sibling grew from baby into child and teenager, the responsibilities became part of 'family life'. The child who is caring did not have or remember any alternative experience of family life. The children and young people had not necessarily chosen to become 'carers' but they had been constrained by the circumstances. It was a natural progression which had evolved to maintain the balance of the family.

It's just part of life now... making sure she's cleaned her teeth and brushed her hair before we go out to school. YOUNG CARER AGED 14

The parents did not realise that the child was 'caring' until he/she had become a major source of support to them.

I miss him [young carer] so much when he goes to school... he is such a help to me and we are very close. CARE RECEIVER, MOTHER

In the families interviewed there were several reasons why the child had become a carer but the underlying reason for all of them was simply that there was no one else to do so at the times when care was needed.

It is just something I do. It has to be done and there is no one else to do it. YOUNG CARER AGED 12

Neighbourly support

There was very little evidence of support from extended family or neighbours. A common theme related by many families was that neighbourly and family support had been plentiful at the onset of illness but gradually withdrew as time passed and the illness remained or worsened. This point was also noted by Aldridge and Becker in *Children Who Care*. Their observations certainly did not reveal a community network of neighbours and friends which the carers could call upon. Amongst the reasons considered for this lack of support was the fact that people may be unwilling to offer help if their commitment might be required for a considerable or undefinable period of time. Aldridge and Becker also stated that 'it could also be due to the fear of, or inability to deal with illness and disability' (*Children Who Care: Inside the World of Young Carers*, Loughborough University, 1993).

This latter point was certainly expressed by adult carers during this research. One adult had received support and offers of help for a short period when she first moved to the neighbourhood but very soon neighbours stopped calling. She felt that she had lost an opportunity to make friends, as the reason they had stopped calling was possibly that they were unable to cope with the nature of the care receiver's disability and were embarrassed that they were no longer offering help.

One-parent families

In one-parent families, when the parent became ill there was no other adult around to offer support in the home so the child became the carer.

When I was first ill she did everything – there was no one else to do it and I was very worried about her having to do so much.
CARE RECEIVER, MOTHER

Well if I don't help her... she'll never get better... and I want her to get better. YOUNG CARER AGED 14

The son has no friends or social life and is kept at home by the mother for emotional support. OBSERVER

Two-parent families

In the two-parent families included in the study, the following reasons were found:

a) In most family situations the able parent has to work, leaving home early in the morning and returning sometimes late in the evening. These are the times when most care tasks need to be performed. If there are small children in the family, the elder child also takes on the role of parenting siblings.

I give the baby his breakfast and take him to mum so she can dress him. YOUNG CARER

Sometimes tasks such as lifting and moving the care receiver required two people and able parents needed assistance from their children.

One adult cannot lift and move another adult unassisted. Someone near at hand is needed to help. ADULT CARER

b) The able parent/adult was frequently away from home for lengthy periods of time.

My dad has to go away to work so I have to look after my mum. He doesn't come home very often. YOUNG CARER AGED 13

c) In one family the reason found was that the able parent was showing signs of depression resulting from their difficulty in coming to terms with the partner's illness, adjusting to the future implications of the illness or readily accepting that their partner needed help. They also showed signs of resentment towards the care receiver for having to remain at home and adopt a new role within the family. The care receiver was still well enough to remain the hub of the family but only with the support of the children.

d) In some families the child feels it is their duty or natural role to take on some of the caring involved in order to give the able parent some respite.

I can't really get out that much because I need to help mum look after dad... she needs to get to have a break. YOUNG CARER AGED 14

I help dad [care receiver] **do the cooking and dishes. Mum can't do it, she gets tired.** YOUNG CARER

Dad needed a break so I stayed with mum while he went away for a few days. YOUNG CARER AGED 15

e) In some families both adults were care receivers. Three families in this situation were identified but it was not possible to talk to them because reservations were expressed by service providers that the nature of the research may be detrimental to the wellbeing of the care receiver or family stability.

Sibling carers

In some families where there is a disabled child, the situation is such that the caring parent is unable to cope alone. Support and assistance from the able siblings are needed at certain times of the day to help with the care of the disabled child, or to look after younger siblings or help around the house while the parent is occupied with the disabled child. Their help may also be needed for certain tasks such as lifting the disabled child, helping them upstairs, getting them in and out of a wheelchair or bath, or helping them go to the toilet.

I can't cope on my own and when he [able son] **goes away I just don't know what we'll do.** MOTHER CARING FOR DISABLED CHILD

If the father was periodically absent in families where there was a disabled child, this substantially increased the role of the able sibling as a carer.

When my dad is away, my mum sometimes gets tired and so I help her look after my sister. YOUNG CARER AGED 12

Dad is away a lot. Mum doesn't really take him out anywhere... she isn't strong enough to push the wheelchair let alone get him in and out of the car. She can't cope when I'm not here. YOUNG CARER AGED 17

In some families the extra responsibilities had become 'part of life.' In others, the caring role had increased to such an extent that the young carer felt resentment at the demands made on them. In one family, the able sibling had imposed the caring role upon herself and would refuse to leave the house or do anything without her disabled sibling.

Such an urge to protect the disabled sibling was observed in other family situations where it had developed into over-protectiveness and the wish to 'parent' or 'do too much' for the brother or sister. Pauline Fairbrother noted that, 'Accepting the responsibilty is often a sibling's way of being noticed, of gaining importance within the family and of seeking assurance of being loved.' (Leach, P.(ed.), *Young Children Under Stress*, VOLCUF, 1992).

3 | WHY ARE YOUNG CARERS 'HIDDEN'?

As described in section 1.4 of the introduction, it took considerable work and many weeks to identify and make contact with the young carers. The evidence of caring by young people is hidden and there are a number of factors that contribute to this.

This chapter looks at how the family's and children's viewpoints contribute to young carers being hidden and also at how service providers' perceptions of young carers and their needs can compound this.

3.1 Perspective of the families and children

Lack of communication

Children expressed embarrassment about their parent's illness and some of the caring responsibilities they perform. When asked they said that they didn't usually talk about their home situation and actively avoided talking to peers and teachers about it. The children want their parents to be like other parents and will go to great lengths to conceal any problems at home. In addition, talking about a situation means acknowledging that it exists and some children may feel that by not talking about their home life the associated problems and anxieties may go away and everything will return to 'normal'.

I don't want people at school to know what he's like. YOUNG CARER AGED 14

Only one of my friends knows, it's not something I talk about and I wouldn't want anyone else to know really. YOUNG CARER AGED 14

This lack of communication is obviously a very difficult issue for schools. If the children go to great lengths to conceal the fact that they are caring then schools may misinterpret any behavioural difficulties, or lack of attendance or achievement and will remain unaware of the child's true situation.

Discussions with health and social workers also highlighted the fact that in most instances a child's contributions to household chores or providing care were not openly discussed with the keyworkers who made home visits, despite it being a significant factor or even a burden in some cases. Adult services often visit when the child is at school and may not even realise that a child has any caring responsibilities. Contributory to this lack of communication was the fact that many care receivers did not regard someone from adult health or social services teams as having any concern with their children's needs.

She [adult health worker] **is very busy. It's not really very easy to talk about these things at clinic. I don't like to take up her time.**
CARE RECEIVER

It was also possible that parents may have felt that to admit their child was caring was to admit inadequacy as a parent and so did not wish to mention it.

Fear and loyalty

Some young carers feel they have a responsibility to hold the family together, particularly those whose parents have a mental health problem, or drug or alcohol related illness, and so will feel a sense of loyalty and obligation to conceal their home situation. Although they all talked candidly in the interviews, some did express guilt at having complained so freely about their situation and the fact that their parent was ill.

Concern was expressed by some parents that to seek help may result in the child being received into care, but this fear was not expressed by any of the children.

5 years ago, when I was finding it difficult to keep the house clean and cope with young children, I asked them [social services] **if I could have some help around the house. The person who answered the phone told me that if I wanted a break they could take my children into care for a few weeks. I put the phone down and didn't dare ask again. I only started to receive the kind of help I really needed after I came out of hospital a short while ago.** CARE RECEIVER, MOTHER

I was so afraid that someone would find out what they were doing. It reached the stage where I didn't dare ask for help in case they took them away and so we just carried on. CARE RECEIVER, MOTHER

However, one younger carer did have anxieties about his mother being taken into residential care or hospital if he was unable to look after her properly. This fear was also expressed by a 15-year-old young carer.

What happens when I can't help? Will she go into hospital? YOUNG CARER

Lack of awareness and information

There was a lack of awareness in some families of types of help available, which had caused them not to seek any help for themselves until the illness had become quite chronic.

I didn't know I was entitled to any help or benefits until I met her.
CARE RECEIVER TALKING ABOUT THE CARE ATTENDANT MANAGER

No one tells you what you are entitled to. You have to find it out as you go along. CARE RECEIVER

If it is difficult for adults to know which agency to turn to for appropriate help and benefits, then how much harder it must be for children to realise that they may be entitled to extra help to relieve their burden.

Although the young carers were unhappy about their parent's illness, they accepted the situation and there was a lack of awareness that life could be different. In fact, one young carer assumed that many other children were in the same situation as himself.

I'm sure lots of my friends have mothers who aren't well but I don't really know who they are... we don't talk about it. YOUNG CARER

None of the children recognised themselves as carers. During discussion at the support group they all said that they did not really like, or associate themselves with the term 'young carer' but couldn't think of another title to describe themselves.

Helping her is just part of life... I don't really remember it being any different. YOUNG CARER AGED 14

I don't see myself as a young carer, just a sister but I suppose I do help her quite a lot. YOUNG CARER AGED 12

3.2 Perceptions of service providers

This section details the responses and reactions of statutory and voluntary service providers encountered during the research.

General perceptions of young carers

In the initial stages of the research, it was apparent that many members of professional and voluntary groups working with children and families, and with adults who have ill health, found it difficult to recognise that young carers existed or to perceive their needs. Comments like, 'Surely it doesn't happen here' or 'It only happens in one-parent families... doesn't it?' were encountered frequently.

In some cases, particularly amongst general practitioners and schools, there was a reluctance to acknowledge that young carers needs cross all boundaries and therefore should be the concern of all agencies. One view expressed both by a practice manager and several teachers was, 'This is a problem for social services. It is not really our job to be concerned with these children.' This poor response from schools and general practitioners has been noted by other research projects. The lack of awareness amongst schools and GPs was also particularly highlighted in a recent evaluation of three regional health authority funded projects in Merseyside. It would appear that the roles performed by young carers are so hidden that until actually confronted with a case it is difficult to accept that children do care.

The research also found many situations where the needs of the care receiver were, rightly or wrongly, placed before those of the child. On several occasions enquiries could proceed no further as the service provider who had given the original details considered that it would be detrimental to the health or mental wellbeing of the care receiver if the researcher were to meet a family where a child was caring.

Education

Schools

In the early weeks of the research, several preliminary approaches were made to schools. It soon became evident that schools had little awareness of young carers and even when they realised the possible issues involved, although they expressed a reserved interest they could not identify any young carers within their schools.

It was apparent throughout the whole of the study that some schools did not regard young carers as their concern. Every senior and primary school was contacted by letter, which fully explained the nature of the project and requested that a simple return slip be completed. Only one primary school identified a young carer. Following this, some senior schools were contacted where it was already known there was a young carer on roll. It was suggested that staff might like the opportunity to discuss the issues involved, in general terms, but this offer was declined.

It was only towards the end of the study, when schools were contacted in order to discuss the possibility of providing support for individual pupils, that staff started to realise that 'caring' affected their pupils educational development and was something with which they should be familiarising themselves with a view to providing appropriate support. Once contact with a head teacher or personal tutor was established, staff were very willing to empathise with the child's situation and to offer help, but it took several months to reach this stage of contact.

It is quite clear from the quotes below that schools need to accept that young carers do exist. Their caring and emotional responsibilities in the home may affect their schooling but the children may not wish their family circumstances to become common knowledge at school. Teachers need to be enabled to recognize indicators which could suggest a child is caring and to know how to approach and handle their needs sensitively (see checklist on pages 66–67).

I know of so many people in my school who have a mum or dad who is seriously ill – for them to say they don't know anyone... that's really irritating. They ought to know and understand what it's like to have a parent who is ill. YOUNG CARER AGED 15

My tutor does understand. She collects information from the other teachers and then visits my mum. YOUNG CARER AGED 14

I was really angry that she should talk about all of this in front of the whole class, I was really upset. YOUNG CARER AGED 15

Education Welfare

Education welfare officers were very committed to the project but only identified four young carers within the area of research, although several more were identified by them outside the area. Usually education welfare officers only become involved when children present behavioural difficulties or have prolonged absences leading to a referral from the school. This could be the reason why they were not aware of the numbers involved. However, two young carers had had prolonged absences from school but had not been referred by the schools to the education welfare service.

Travellers Education Service

The Travellers Education Service were in regular contact with children of travellers and were able to identify instances of children caring. Travellers needs may be compounded by the fact that, in cases where they have no fixed address, they have no direct access to services such as GPs or regular schooling.

Social services

Initially, some social workers took time to assimilate the issues involved around young carers, particularly if they were members of adult service teams. However, once they understood the nature and purpose of the research, the level of co-operation was high. The aims of the research were disseminated by means of team meetings which in turn led to other teams and departments who may have had a contribution. A large majority of the referrals were received from social work teams. In particular, a large number were received from the Care Attendant Scheme

Manager who is responsible for assessing care receivers' requirements for extra support in the home. She was very aware of the issues concerning young carers to the extent that she was tailoring services to the adult client to reflect the needs of a child whenever possible.

Some social workers had suspected that a child was caring but because their client was the care receiver, they had little opportunity or reason to make contact with the child and were unsure what to do about the situation. Concern was expressed that these children needed support but were falling through the 'gap' between adult and children's services.

The children and families team were instrumental in commissioning this research. They were very aware that children were caring but had no means of knowing which children had caring responsibilities or how to start identifying them. Children were only referred to them when a crisis situation had developed. Families who need support but are not in crisis could feel threatened if a children's social worker suggested an assessment.

Liaison between adult services and children's services was not facilitated on an ongoing basis at the time of research and even if it had been, because of the general lack of awareness of young carers and the hidden nature of these children, it does not necessarily follow that such contact would have revealed the young carers.

Since the start of this research adult and children's teams have become more aware of young carers and their needs and adult teams now refer any families in which a child may be needing support to the children's team. Where possible, extra support from adult teams is being given to care receivers in order to relieve the burden placed on the child.

Comments about social services from the families were, on the whole, quite complimentary. However, the main complaints were that there wasn't enough support in the home or that it wasn't what the family really needed.

He [social worker] visits us once a fortnight. He's very good at his job but he may have to come less often in the future. He's very busy. CARE RECEIVER

The social worker said that we could get physio and someone in once a week to help and all these wonderful things she was going to organise, but it turns out we just have someone once a week to do the shopping. We have had to pay for a private cleaner to come in because I can't do it all. YOUNG CARER

We get a lot of help really, but it's still not enough. I worry about the effect this is having on her and I want someone to help her. CARE RECEIVER

Why is it that the bank and BT can send me letters in Braille and
the social services and health can't? I have to ask my children to
read it... It isn't very satisfactory and there are some things I would
rather they didn't have to know about. CARE RECEIVER

Health services

We had been asking for help for a long time but nothing happened
until just recently. We only used to get help occasionally. Now we
still don't get any extra help when my father is at home so I still
have to help on those days because it needs two of us. YOUNG
CARER

A local resource 'Information Exchange' (see Appendix 1) was very
instrumental in spreading information about this research to health
workers. It was also possible to make contact with many voluntary groups
through this resource. However, after this initial contact, maintaining the
impetus proved to be more difficult. The initial contacts made with
school doctors, nurses and health visitors proved not to be a good source
of identifying possible young carers.

General practitioners

As described in the introduction to this section, general practitioners
were unforthcoming and did not really participate in the project. Practice
managers did not see young carers needs as a GP's responsibility and
unfortunately, despite repeated requests, no practices responded.

However, towards the end of the research, one city practice agreed to
run a month's trial. The GPs were asked to keep the issue of children
caring to the front of their minds whenever seeing patients with long-
term illnesses and to try and ascertain whether any of their clients who
were parents may be being cared for by their children. Numbers only
were requested so that there should be no anxieties about patient
confidentiality. A nil response was received, despite the fact that some of
the children and families already identified were registered at the practice.

One young carer who was feeling particularly depressed arranged for
an appointment with the GP but unfortunately did not meet with a
sympathetic ear.

I went to the doctor and told him I was tired and tried to talk to
him. He didn't believe me... He was so annoying... there was no
point trying to talk to him. YOUNG CARER

Health visitors and community nurses

A number of health visitors and community nurses were contacted and all of them seemed to accept that young carers existed. On initial contact, some acknowledged that they already knew of some young carers and were willing to participate in the study. However, only one positive referral was received from a health visitor throughout the research and lack of time prevented any further follow up.

School doctors and nurses

The same pattern was repeated here. The school doctors and nurses recognised and accepted the issues relating to young carers and felt the research project was of value but were only able to identify one young carer.

Macmillan and Home Care Nurses

Both teams were aware of young carers and their needs but had no clients with children caring during the period of research.

Winchester Specialist Team for People with Learning Disabilities

This specialist team were aware of the existence of some young carers and the problems facing them, particularly sibling carers. Needs had been recognised amongst some families and support was being offered to one family where the level of care was posing a strain on the young carer.

Manager for the Young Physically Disabled (health)

A large number of referrals came from this manager. She was very aware of the issues involved and had been very concerned about many family situations but, until the research commenced, there had been no one to assess young carers' needs. She did not usually see the children themselves as visits to clients were during school hours. When she did see them it was not possible to talk to them on their own so, although she suspected that the child was 'caring', it was difficult to establish exactly which responsibilities were being undertaken by the child. Families did not discuss their children's role at any time. This could be because they had not recognised their child's needs or did not wish to or think it appropriate to raise the matter. Where it was clear that a child was undertaking a high level of caring, extra support was given to the care receiver whenever possible to reduce the burden on the child.

Voluntary agencies

Both local and national support groups were contacted by telephone. Had there been more time available, it would have been desirable to make contact with more. Those contacted included MIND, Multiple Sclerosis Society, Mencap, Cancerlink, Schizophrenia Society and Arthritis Care.

Not many of the voluntary support or self-help groups approached were aware that children may be carers. In instances where there was a level of awareness, it was realised that this could be a very sensitive and difficult topic to mention in newsletters or group meetings without having something positive to offer in return. Referrals were received from two groups only.

Patterns of awareness

It was evident as the project progressed, that most agencies contacted had become more aware of young carers' needs and, as a result, their perceptions changed. They became involved in discussing ways forward and started to consider young carers' needs as a separate issue. For some families, some of the extra help they needed is already being put into place but their needs, and those of their young carers, may still have remained hidden if this project had not been commissioned and funded. This seems to underline the need for initial and continuing surveys of this kind in all areas of the country.

Current services provided to young carers

The following services were found to have been put into place either before the research period commenced, or during it, as a result of increasing levels of awareness in service providers promoted by the research.

● Care services are now being provided to the care receiver in all the homes which were visited. The needs of the young carer have been assessed informally in three homes and as a result extra provisions made to the care receiver.

● In one home, extra care hours have been provided to reduce the level of care being performed by the young carer. This was put into place during the project.

● In another home where the young carer is supportive but is only 8-years-old, a lifeline link has been provided. This is used via a special telephone. Help can be summoned at any time of the night or day by pressing a red button on the telephone or on a pendant or bracelet worn by the care receiver. The young carer has been taught how to use it if a crisis occurs and this has proved very reassuring to him.

● One senior school has arranged for the child's personal tutor to make visits to the family home to discuss the child's work with the parent. This has proved most helpful to the parent in maintaining a link with the school and her child's progress.

● Support from the Home Tutors team was provided to another pupil.

Home Tutors provide a full range of education for children who are, for good reason, unable to attend school for a period of time.

● Several pupils may be provided with an accompanying letter to explain extenuating circumstances which may affect their coursework and exam grades in GCSEs.

● One child was receiving counselling at the time of research and another three had done so in the past.

4 | ASPECTS OF CARING

It was discovered that the young carers were undertaking a range of tasks which included practical and physical assistance, as well as coping with the associated emotional stress and responsibility.

These tasks were the same whether a child lived in a rural area or in the city. They also reflected findings from research projects in other parts of the country and those made in an exploratory cross-national study *Young Carers in Europe* (S. Becker (ed.).

Caring for a physically disabled parent or sibling obviously entails tasks of a more physical nature, particularly where the care receiver has little or no mobility. The caring responsibilities undertaken by children whose parents had a mental health problem, or drug or alcohol related problem were often less visible and included tasks such as watching for the parent's safety, reminding them of medication times and parenting younger, able brothers and sisters.

The range of tasks and responsibilities undertaken by the young carers included shopping, budgeting, cashing giros, cleaning the house and preparing meals. More intimate tasks such as toileting, emptying a commode and bathing were also undertaken by some. Some children collected prescriptions and ensured parents took their medication at correct times.

Communicating on behalf of the parent, watching out for parental safety and parenting younger siblings were three additional areas of responsibility recorded. Emotionally, responsibilities included counselling the parent, giving companionship and in some cases parenting the parent. The words of the young carers documented throughout this chapter describe their responsibilities.

4.1 Practical tasks and responsibilities

Cooking

I sit and think... what's in the freezer that we can eat tonight?
YOUNG CARER AGED 14

I used to do all the cooking but my sister does it now. YOUNG CARER AGED 13

We share the jobs... I do all the cleaning and he [brother] does the cooking. YOUNG CARER AGED 12

Eastenders clashes with making the dinner... I sit down to watch it and then mum comes in and starts to do some of it and I feel really guilty. YOUNG CARER AGED 14

Housework

I do the hoovering for mum as she gets very tired. YOUNG CARER AGED 8

I share the jobs with my sister but as she has got her 'A' levels this year she needs to do her school work even more than me so I do more at the moment. She goes away next year and so it'll just be me and mum might get worse. YOUNG CARER

I'd like a robot to help my dad in the house. YOUNG CARER AGED 10

I used to do all the cleaning but now we have someone to help so I don't need to do so much. At least I don't have to wash the kitchen floor so much now. YOUNG CARER AGED 14

Shopping

I like to push the trolley in the supermarket... It's too heavy for mum... but people get in the way and I bang into them and then they think I'm being naughty but I'm trying to help. YOUNG CARER

I'm going to do all the Christmas shopping because mum can't go out to the shops. YOUNG CARER AGED 14

I collect all her money and get her prescriptions. YOUNG CARER AGED 14

They [home help] always forget something or I find the cupboards empty, so I run up to the shop to get things when we've run out. YOUNG CARER AGED 14

Out and about

I'm not going to use a wheelchair, I can't do it... I've thought about it but I can't bring myself to use one so we don't go out together. I know she wants me to go out with her and it's hard for her. She does any shopping we need. CARE RECEIVER

We can't go many places with him [father]... it's hard work. YOUNG CARER

I hold on to mum when we go out so she won't fall over – she uses the baby's buggy to help her when I'm not there. I don't know what

she'll do when he's too big for the buggy and I'm not there.
YOUNG CARER

Parenting younger siblings

Her mum would praise her by saying, 'she is a little mother' and 'I don't know what I'd do without her'. She was expected to amuse both her disabled brother and the baby directly after school and play with the disabled brother until bedtime. She was often left to carry and hold the baby when out, even though it was a struggle. OBSERVER

There are five children and the eldest looks after the others.
OBSERVER

I give the baby his breakfast and take him to mum so she can dress him. YOUNG CARER

The child was left alone at the site for days on end to look after the younger child. Other travellers were nearby but not in the same van. OBSERVER

Responsibility for parents

In a family where parents had a drug or alcohol related problem, instances were observed where the child became responsible for their safety and welfare.

She used to guide her parents home at night. They were incapable of doing it on their own. She probably put them to bed and sorted out all the other things that needed doing when she got them through the door as well. OBSERVER

Another young carer had exerted authority over her mother to ensure her illness did not regress.

She used to have agrophobia, so I make sure that she goes out of the flat every day for a little while, but she can't walk far because she doesn't have the energy. YOUNG CARER AGED 14

Physical care

My mum needs help to lift him [father]... she can't do it on her own.
YOUNG CARER AGED 14

He [brother] can walk with a lot of assistance. I can just about walk him by myself but my mother can't. He's too heavy. If he starts going one way... we all topple. YOUNG CARER AGED 17

I take him [brother] to the toilet four or five times a day and move him around whenever it's needed. Nobody has taught me how to lift but you learn fairly fast... you soon find out what hurts and what doesn't. YOUNG CARER AGED 17

Sometimes she [care receiver] can't help and it's very difficult to slide her on to the lift. YOUNG CARER AGED 12

Personal care and toileting

Not surprisingly this was the area of care about which the children expressed most embarrassment or a wish to stop. Families were found where sons were helping mothers with toileting needs and daughters their fathers, including emptying and cleaning commodes. For a teenager, the body is a particularly sensitive subject and it cannot be easy for these young carers to perform such tasks. For some, it has resulted in a feeling of resentment towards their parent. For the parent, the loss of dignity involved in having to rely on your child for toileting needs must be equally humiliating to bear.

The younger sister was expected to help her mother lift her older disabled brother in and out of the bath and watch him, even after he had reached puberty. OBSERVER

I help her when she goes to the loo... she can't do it on her own. YOUNG CARER AGED 12

I don't like having to change my sister if she has wet herself but I do it to help mum if she is ill or very tired. YOUNG CARER AGED 12

I couldn't cope without him [young carer]. I'm not strong enough to put him [father] on the toilet on my own. ADULT CARER, MOTHER

Many of the above quotes came from families where there is already an element of homecare being provided by health or social services. Despite the support received from home-help or careworkers, the assistance given by the children was still heavily relied upon on a daily basis to keep the family and home running. No one had previously asked any of the children how they felt or whether they had any need for support.

4.2 Emotional issues

When I go to bed at night, I can shut the door and forget everything. YOUNG CARER AGED 14

The emotional demands of caring can be quite exhausting, even for adult carers. Caring for someone who has a disability or long-term illness is an ongoing commitment to which there may seem to be no end, unless the care receiver goes into residential care or dies. A parent with mental health problems may exhibit unpredictable behaviour patterns, which can be emotionally stressful and difficult for a child or young person to understand. This is also true in families where the parent has a drug or alcohol related problem.

A child or young person does not choose to care but is compelled to do so by the circumstances. Most expressed the desire to see their parent or sibling well again.

I wish I could make dad's leg better. YOUNG CARER AGED 10

I know if I don't look after her she'll never get better and I want her to get better. YOUNG CARER AGED 14

They also expressed resentment and anger at the illness striking someone they loved.

I hate it when people make fun of brain-damaged children, they don't know what they're really like. YOUNG CARER AGED 12

I feel so angry about my sister... Why her?... It's not fair – why not somebody else's sister... why does it have to be her? YOUNG CARER AGED 14

This research found that although most of the children showed a commitment to caring for their parent or sibling, some also expressed an underlying resentment that they should be placed in this situation.

Why me... why should I have to do this? YOUNG CARER AGED 13

The following pages of quotes illustrate the children's feelings about their parent's illness, their emotional burden and their own need to talk and be listened to.

Dealing with the illness or disability

All children who care have a common link in that a member of their family has a chronic or long-term illness or disability. Whether or not the child is caring he/she is still affected emotionally, to a greater or lesser degree, by having to come to terms with this.

I don't know what is going to happen to her... I don't think she will go mad but I just don't know. YOUNG CARER

It's not just the caring that affects you... in fact we're a very close family and we all pull together. What really gets you is the worry of

it all, having a parent who is ill and seeing them in such a state...
of course it's upsetting, you think about it a lot. Someone who is
so close to you and desperately ill is pretty hard to deal with.
FORMER YOUNG CARER

I used to get upset when people stared – they don't know what to
say. YOUNG CARER AGED 12

When I first heard mum had MS I was upset... then I thought, will
I get it too? They tell me I won't but I still worry sometimes.
FORMER YOUNG CARER

I feel different to other people because my sister has Downs
Syndrome. YOUNG CARER AGED 14

She [mother] looks so pale and ill, you just don't know what to do.
Sometimes she's in so much pain, I've thought, 'What can I do?',
but there is nothing I can do to help the pain. YOUNG CARER

I don't talk to my mum about it but I know all about it – I've read
about it and seen the ads. YOUNG CARER

(Multiple Sclerosis Society fundraising advertisements were the basis of
information for two children in this research. They were the cause of a
great deal of distress and anxiety about the future for these children. This
highlights the fact that if children are not provided with adequate
information about their parent's illness then they may learn about it from
inappropriate sources.)

The responsibility

One child gave her mother a high level of emotional support.

Mum [care receiver] might be upset when I get in after a hard day
at school and I have to calm her down... but you really don't feel
like counselling her. YOUNG CARER

Another was anxious for his mother's safety and one young carer
expressed anxieties about the future implications of her sister's disability.

I get frightened when I hear a bump in the night. It might be mum
falling over. YOUNG CARER

I understand that she [disabled sister] needs to go away
sometimes to give us all a break but I couldn't bear to think of her
going away for ever... but what happens when she leaves school.
Who will watch her all the time? YOUNG CARER AGED 14

Some young carers showed anxiety about the able caring parent and a need to protect them from the excessive demands of the care receiver.

I need to help mum look after dad, she needs a break. She couldn't cope if she had to stay in with him all the time. YOUNG CARER AGED 14

She cannot cope on her own and I leave home next year. I just don't know what she will do. YOUNG CARER AGED 17

4.3 Isolation and the need to talk

You [researcher] **are the first person who has ever asked me how I feel.** YOUNG CARER AGED 15

It was very apparent that all the young carers needed to talk and some poured out all their pent-up feelings during the interviews. Some of the feelings expressed showed a desperate need to be heard and believed and for their role as a carer to be recognised.

I talked to my friends mother about some things but there isn't really anyone else to talk to. I couldn't believe it when I heard about you [researcher]**. I wish I'd been told about you sooner.** YOUNG CARER AGED 15

I hate to say it but we do know more about the situation than the people who try to help... Why don't they listen to us... I'd like to go and tell them all what it's really like. YOUNG CARER AGED 17

The people who come to talk to dad are nice but I have to make myself scarce... go upstairs out of the way so I don't get a chance to say anything. I couldn't say anything in front of him anyway. YOUNG CARER AGED 14

I'd like to know why my mum is ill and I'd like someone who really knows all about it to tell me. I can't talk to mum about it, she gets too upset. YOUNG CARER

I like talking to him [counsellor]**, it helps.** YOUNG CARER AGED 13

Some of the parents (mostly the caring parent) were very relieved that at last someone had raised the subject of their children caring. Three of the care receivers were pleased someone was talking to their child. Two care receivers refused to discuss or accept the fact that their child was caring despite the extensive role played by them.

The children all expressed a sense of isolation due to not being able to talk to their friends about family life, and the feeling that they were the only ones in such a situation.

I talk to my friends a bit but they don't really understand. YOUNG CARER AGED 14

I'm sure there are other children at my school who look after their mums, I expect I know them but they never talk about it to me. YOUNG CARER

At school, sometimes people ask questions about my sister... why is she like she is? They don't understand... it's difficult to explain all the time. YOUNG CARER AGED 12

5 | THE EFFECT OF CARING ON THE CHILD'S LIFE

This chapter examines the effect caring can have on the lives of young carers, including its impact on the relationship between young carer and care receiver, on the social life and personal development of young carers and on their school life. It also describes how caring as a child can have a lasting emotional influence through into adulthood.

In all of the families interviewed, except one, it was observed that the children were experiencing some degree of emotional strain. In the one family where the caring did not appear to be imposing any strain on the children, the care receiver's illness was of a moderate nature.

5.1 Relationships between young carers and care receivers

Transfer of role and the false maturity observed in most young carers can lead to a change or destabilising of the relationship between young carer and care receiver. The role of caring, together with the underlying emotional burden, causes young carers to assume a mantle of responsibility not usually associated with childhood. In effect, many of the children interviewed were parents to their parents.

Only three of the young carers interviewed did not show signs of false maturity and they were presenting behavioural difficulties at school and were out of parental control at home. The children mostly behaved in a far more mature way than would be expected in peers of their age group. Most were very quiet and self-contained and even the younger ones performed a lot of self-care tasks.

Some adult care receivers felt they were losing their parental role, perhaps resenting their enforced dependency, and as a result became authoritarian and overdemanding towards their children in an attempt to maintain a presence or control over their lives. In some families where the demands placed on the young carer were unreasonable, this led to resentment and caused dysfunction between the child and carer receiver. In three of the homes the young carer and care receiver were observed to be continually shouting at each other.

He doesn't ask for things, he demands them. He never says thank you. YOUNG CARER

She always waits until I'm doing something else and then shouts for me to get a drink or something... it is so annoying. YOUNG CARER

He waits until I've started my homework and then asks for something... It's always something unimportant and he does it over and over again. YOUNG CARER

In these situations the able adult carer was very anxious about the effect such demanding behaviour may be having on their child but the situation had existed for so long that they seemed unable to do anything about it.

This change in parent/child roles often led to the parent's inability to exert authority over the child.

I like to go out at night... I tell my mum I'm going somewhere that I'm not and then I go up the road with the gang – if she knew... she'd stop me. YOUNG CARER

I can never be a 'mother' to them again. I've lost that special child/parent relationship for ever. It took me some time to accept this... now we live as equals. It can cause problems... it can be hard to exert authority but I do try and discuss everything with them. CARE RECEIVER, NOW FULLY RECOVERED

In some families the illness or caring tasks had never been openly discussed, even where the situation and the tasks involved were imposing obvious strain on all family members. This inability to talk to each other was also causing an uneasy and, in one case, dysfunctional relationship between child and care receiver.

I just don't talk to my mum very much... there's nothing to talk about. YOUNG CARER

I can talk to my mum a bit but I can't really say how I feel to her. YOUNG CARER AGED 15

Anger and guilt were also expressed by some of the children.

There comes a point when you just want to leave and you think you just can't take anymore... then you feel guilty because you think you should be at home with her all the time. YOUNG CARER

I still feel so angry that she wasn't 'there' when I needed her most. FORMER YOUNG CARER

5.2 The parents' perspective

Whilst parents often agree that the children should not have to care, many actually want them to continue whilst, at the same time, acknowledging the unacceptability of their children performing certain, more intimate tasks. J. ALDRIDGE, S. BECKER, C. DEARDEN, *PARTNERS IN CARING*, CARERS NATIONAL ASSOCIATION, 1994

Some of the parents, both able parents and care receivers, admitted that asking their child to undertake caring responsibilities, particularly those of a personal nature, may not be ideal but could see no alternative or, in some cases, did not want a 'stranger' to help with personal needs.

I know it's not ideal but we manage the way we are. CARE RECEIVER

Some parents were concerned about the effect of caring on their child's life but needed the child's practical assistance to maintain a stable family life. They were aware that no amount of protection could prevent the child from experiencing emotional anguish about the illness or disability.

I worry about the effect all this is having on her. ABLE PARENT

In some families the able parent or care receiver did not really recognise that their child was caring or thought that it was appropriate for the children to give support, even when the child was undertaking a very high level of caring responsibilities. One parent declared that if the children were old enough then they should carry out all the care tasks.

I leave it all to them now they're old enough. ABLE PARENT

Two parents admitted readily that they needed their child for support and could not cope without them.

I can't cope on my own and when he leaves home... I just won't be able to manage. I don't know what will happen. ABLE PARENT

I miss him so much when he goes to school... he is such a help to me and we are very close. CARE RECEIVER, MOTHER

Some families commented that the research was very necessary, particularly if it resulted in extra support being provided for their children. On the whole, this type of comment came from the able adult carer as opposed to the care receiver.

I am so pleased somebody is listening to them. Nobody has offered them anything before. ABLE PARENT

5.3 Sibling carers

Caring for a sibling with a disability can have similar consequences to those of a child caring for his or her parent. If too many demands are made by the parents for assistance from the able child, this can lead to resentment and dysfunction in family relationships. Such dysfunction was observed in one of the families where the able child was expected to give a substantial amount of support.

Underlying emotional anxieties were also evident in sibling carers and in one instance the child's social development was severely restricted by caring responsibilities.

5.4 Social life and personal development

A general observation frequently made by those in direct contact with the young carers was that they often seemed to be isolated and did not always mix freely with other children. The maturity they developed through caring often remained with them in other situations. Some children were overbearing with their peers, which caused conflict at school leading to rejection. Others were very quiet and withdrawn whilst a third group displayed disruptive behaviour.

Many of the young teenage carers were unable to develop a social life of their own. They were unwilling to leave the care receiver unattended or to ask the able parent to take them anywhere. This proved to be a particular problem for families living in a rural area where there is a lack of public transport.

It isn't easy to go out because he has to leave her while he drives us to places. YOUNG CARER AGED 15

I don't like to ask him [adult carer] **to take me places so I don't go unless I can stay over for the night.** YOUNG CARER AGED 15

Embarrassment about their parent's illness often made them reluctant to invite friends home or to discuss family matters with their peer groups.

I can't ask friends home, not when dad's there. YOUNG CARER AGED 14

Not a lot of people know I've got a brother because they don't really meet him. So I do have to explain a lot why I can't go out. YOUNG CARER AGED 17

The social and personal development of some children were severely restricted by the demands placed upon them by their parents.

On several occasions, when the child wished to go out to a friend's house, she was denied this request. OBSERVER

I say I'm off now and they say... no you can't we're going out... you have to stay in and look after him. I wouldn't mind so much if I got some advance warning or consideration. YOUNG CARER

The mother was cared for by the daughter, who became agrophobic herself. Now she has left home but the pattern is being repeated with the younger son. OBSERVER

In one family where the care receiver suffered from a mental health problem, it was observed that the mother needed her child to be with her at all times and was afraid to be left alone.

The son has no social life or friends and is kept at home by his mother for emotional support. OBSERVER

Some of the families contacted admitted there were financial constraints caused by the illness and that this limited opportunities for family outings. Family outings were also limited because of the difficulties encountered by the care receiver in getting about.

I can't take her anywhere. I wouldn't have the energy to do anything if I did go out and not knowing from one day to the next how I'll be feeling makes it very difficult to plan anything. CARE RECEIVER, MOTHER

His best friend lives in the next village but he doesn't see him very often because it's too far for me to take him. CARE RECEIVER, MOTHER

They miss going to the park. I can't play football with them anymore. CARE RECEIVER, FATHER

A self imposed 'caring curfew' was expressed by a former young carer who never went anywhere without leaving a contact telephone number and always ensured that he came home in time to help.

Before I went out, I always let them know where I was going to be and got back in time to help if I was needed. FORMER YOUNG CARER

5.5 School life and education

Generally, school is seen as an escape by many young carers, a place where they can forget the worries and stresses of home life. Most of them do not wish the school to know about their home situation and often go to great lengths to make excuses for lateness or poor work rather than admit their parent is ill and needs their help.

Lack of communication

Most of the children expressed embarrassment at the idea of telling their friends or teachers about their home situation and chose not to discuss the matter at school.

My best friend knows but I wouldn't want anyone else to know... they wouldn't understand. YOUNG CARER AGED 14

I don't want people at school to know what he's like. YOUNG CARER AGED 14

It's hard to talk to the teacher when everyone is listening. YOUNG CARER AGED 15

Amongst the families met, some care receivers admitted that they felt unable to control their emotions sufficiently to talk to the school about their illness and so the school had no idea anything was wrong. Others were physically unable to get to the school for occasions such as parents' evenings.

My mum can't visit school... It's too far for her to walk and there are too many stairs and corridors. YOUNG CARER

My mum couldn't get to school for parents' evening... my tutors were very cross and just didn't understand. YOUNG CARER AGED 15

These quotes underline why young carers are so 'hidden' at school and why, when the home situation does become known to staff, a very sensitive and confidential approach is needed.

Special needs and underachieving

Six of the children interviewed had difficulties with learning. Of those six, one had been seen by an educational psychologist to assess behavioural difficulties and three others by the child guidance service for counselling and family therapy. Two were assessed as having special needs.

A further three children admitted that they were not able to apply enough time and effort to their work and were therefore not getting the results they had hoped for. This underachievement was occurring at a very critical time in their educational life.

I want to achieve, I want to do well. I was thinking of studying medicine but I think that's probably out of the question now... I do try hard but nobody seems to realise what is going on at home. They say, 'You're not doing your best'... but it is my best. YOUNG CARER AGED 15

I don't always feel my homework is good enough. I have to rush to get it done. YOUNG CARER AGED 15

Well I just don't do my homework. I don't have the time, then it all piles up and I have to do it in a rush. YOUNG CARER AGED 14

It wouldn't really help if I stayed on late at school to do my work because things would still have to be done when I get home. Things like cooking the tea can't wait. YOUNG CARER AGED 15

Other people go home and have everything done for them and they still find it hard to cope with the work, and there's me having so much to help with and I still have only the same amount of time to complete my work and I'm expected to do as well – that's what I think is really unfair. YOUNG CARER

Pupil/teacher relationships

Most of the young carers interviewed felt that teachers would not be able to empathise with their situation, even if they were made aware of the issues surrounding it. Many expressed the concern that if they did confide in the teacher then details of their home situation may be disclosed to other members of the class. Opportunities to speak to the teacher in private were also difficult to come by.

My form tutor understands but I don't think that the other teachers are aware or understand the consequences of having a mother who is ill. We don't get asked if we have any difficulties. They only know if you tell them and even then... I don't think they understand just what it's like. YOUNG CARER

It's difficult to talk to the teachers... it's not easy to explain... it's always in the corridor or in the class. I just don't tell them. YOUNG CARER AGED 15

Absences

One young carer is frequently ten or fifteen minutes late for school because he needs to carry out various care tasks before leaving home in the morning. This used to cause him a great deal of anxiety and he constantly made up excuses to explain his lateness. Now that the school is aware of the situation, no comment is made on his late arrival and he is also being given extra help in the home.

Two other young carers have had longer absences from school varying from between three to six weeks. In both cases these absences were attributed to stress related illness.

5.6 Long term effects

Former young carers

She stopped being my mother a long time ago... she is just a person who happens to be my mother. FORMER YOUNG CARER

Throughout the investigations, it became increasingly clear that the effects of caring as a child can have a lasting impact throughout adult life. Adults ranging in age from 22 to mid 50s, who had cared for a parent or sibling when they were a child, were encountered during the research period.

The original research design aimed to limit contact to former young carers up to the age of 25, so people above this age were not actively sought. However, adults of all ages made contact of their own accord and recounted their experiences and feelings about caring when they were children. Following a discussion about the research, the researcher was approached by several people acknowledging that the issues and needs which had just been described were indeed part of their own childhood experience but they had never really thought of themselves as carers before, nor confronted the impact it had had on their lives.

Other people already known to the researcher related their own childhood experiences when they discovered the subject of the research.

Two people experienced a head on confrontation with feelings and emotions that had been denied for many years, and the descriptions of their childhoods were very emotional. One woman, now in her 30s, cared for her parent who not only had a physical disability but also mental health problems. She was also responsible for performing the general household tasks and cooked for the whole family. She was aware that these responsibilities had restricted her own social life and education. Even now she finds it difficult to feel affection for her parent and has experienced difficulties making friends and establishing relationships throughout life. She had always thought there must be something wrong with her but had never attributed it to missing out on an important part of childhood development. She described the feeling of realisation that perhaps it was the responsibilities of caring and the restrictions imposed by them which had left an emotional mark on her as a *dawning of light*.

Another woman of similar age acknowledged that she was finally confronting feelings she had previously kept hidden in the back of her mind. She had not cared for her parents in a physical way but had shouldered the emotional responsibility of holding the family together. Together with her younger sisters, she remembers it as a bewildering time for all of them. Her father had been chronically ill and her mother had a severe alcohol problem.

It still hurts and I still feel angry when I think about it... She was never 'there' when I needed her but I always had to look after her when she was having a bad day.

She too acknowledged that her childhood responsibilities and dysfunctional relationship with both parents had affected her social development and she has found it hard to form relationships in adult life. She is aware that in the past she was always looking for total perfection in both herself and her partner. Only recently has she started to find it easier to trust people and form relationships. Also, it is only recently that she has been able to discuss what happened in her childhood with her mother, who no longer, happily, has any problems. She cannot remember ever discussing the circumstances and events of family life with her sisters when they were children. The situation had existed but was never openly acknowledged by them.

A former male young carer related similar experiences of being unable to form relationships easily. He remembers being kept home from school to look after his mother (his father worked away from home and when around was unable to cope with his wife's illness). When he did go to school he was either too tired to work or so far behind that he kept failing. He still feels great resentment towards his mother for the demands she and his father made on him and his older brother.

Another person who had cared for a younger disabled sibling was still affected by the impact it had had on her during her childhood and found herself feeling resentful towards her own child's freedom.

Positive effects of caring

During this research, members of the reference group asked if any positive effects of caring as a child could be found and highlighted. Unlike Saul Becker in *Children Who Care*, who found children expressing a sense of being needed and of fulfilment from their caring roles, none of the children interviewed in this research expressed such feelings.

Only one child gained comfort from helping his mother but at the same time longed for her to get better.

I like helping... she doesn't get tired if I help. If she gets tired it makes her ill again. YOUNG CARER

The question was also raised whether evidence could be found which indicated that having to care at an early age resulted in the child becoming more caring outside the family. No detailed research by other projects could be found to prove or disprove this point and no evidence was collected during this research. Two of the former young carers interviewed for this research work in the caring professions but three do not. One former young carer did express this viewpoint:

It makes you appreciate how other disabled people feel... I can relate to them more and am not afraid to talk to them in the street.
FORMER YOUNG CARER

6 | CONCLUSIONS

This chapter bases its conclusions on the key findings of the research in HCCSSD, Winchester area, the observations of other research projects and relevant legislation and policy statements.

6.1 Summary of key findings

• **An unexpectedly high number of young carers were found.** In addition to sole young carers, a considerable number who were caring in a supportive role were also found, as were those helping to care for a sibling with a disability. Some young carers who were in a two-parent family where an able adult was present were in fact the main carers. Some children were found to be caring for more than one family member.

• **Many professionals working with children, in particular schools and general practitioners, seemed unaware of the existence of young carers and their needs.** Because of this lack of awareness, the young carers were 'hidden' and it took a long time to identify them. However, once the young carers and their families were contacted, those interviewed welcomed the chance to talk to someone who was concerned about their own needs. Social services were the most common source of referral whereas young carers were not apparent to most schools and general practitioners.

• **The spectrum of needs found, both practical, physical and emotional, raised far more issues for a wider range of service providers than expected.** In addition to traditional caring tasks such as practical and personal care, many young carers are also giving emotional support and are responsible for looking after younger siblings. The full spectrum of needs and issues identified can be found in Appendix 6.

• **More children caring for a relative with a 'visible' illness, eg. a physical disability, were identified than those caring for a parent with a mental health problem, or drugs or alcohol related illness.** It proved difficult to identify the needs of young carers in these latter categories. There is a requirement for more in depth study in this area, to be followed up by appropriate support for this particular group of young carers.

• **Services are being provided for the care receiver but the needs of young carers are not being directly addressed.** The perception that a family could not be approached if it was thought that it would be detrimental to the care receiver needs to be addressed, otherwise there is a danger that the needs of the young carer will always be placed after the needs of the care receiver.

● **There needs to be more communication and collaboration between agencies and between services for adults and services for children.** All except two of the families identified by this research were already known to one or more agencies. What was not known, in so many of the cases, was that the children in these families were caring. Additionally, support for the care receiver from the adult teams of the appropriate agency could help resolve some of the needs of the young carer.

● **The issue of acceptable and unacceptable levels of care needs to be addressed by anyone proposing to work with young carers.** In addition to considering the effect that caring responsibilities may be having on a child's wellbeing and personal or educational development, the needs and wishes of the young carers themselves need to be in line with the principles of the Children Act. Each situation will also be affected by individual family circumstances.

● **Management of the research by a voluntary agency enabled it to remain independent of statutory agencies.** This meant that the research could be conducted autonomously and helped facilitate access to all agencies and families. The involvement of The Children's Society also emphasised that it was the children who were the focus of attention.

● **Illness or impairment can strike any family at any time so there will always be a need to identify new young carers and their specific needs, if local authorities are going to adhere to the legislative guidelines.** It is going to take a long time before these children readily seek help for themselves. Identifying them and ensuring that they receive the support they each need will remain a sensitive area of work.

6.2 Young carers' needs

General

Caring can affect a child's educational, social and personal development. It can also affect them emotionally, not only in childhood but through into adult life. It is clear from the comments made by young carers throughout this report that the support they require should be provided by different agencies, since help and support is required in a number of forms. Young carers expressed a need to talk, to be listened to and to know their needs are recognised and understood.

Young carers have needs which:

- are complex and differ according to each family situation;

- need to be considered independently from those of the care receiver;

- have implications for service provisions which are the responsibility of health and social services (both adults' and children's resources), education, youth services and voluntary agencies;

- require a sensitive and confidential approach;

- can have a long-term impact on their childhood which remains in later life.

Provision of information

Young carers need to be given a suitable explanation about the care receiver's illness. They may need to know the reasons behind any changes in parental roles or household routines and, in particular, about any decisions made regarding help for the care receiver which may affect them. The amount of information provided should be governed by the child's ability to understand but given whenever appropriate. Information should be updated if the situation changes.

Children should also be given access to information on appropriate services for the care receiver and for themselves, and some families may need to be given advice about which benefits they may be eligible to claim.

An advocate may be needed if a child is unable to articulate his or her needs clearly.

Counselling and emotional support

This needs to be given in two forms. Families need to be encouraged and enabled to discuss their situation freely amongst themselves and to build upon their strengths. Appropriate counselling is also needed by some young carers and should be made available if it is requested or considered beneficial for the child. Counselling services should also be available if the parent dies, not only for bereavement but also to help the child come to terms with the loss of role.

Practical support

Practical support may be required from health and social services, in the form of extra provision in the home for the care receiver to reduce the level of responsibility undertaken by the child and to protect the child's own physical and psychological wellbeing.

For young carers in rural areas extra help with transport, when appropriate, may reduce some of the restrictions on their lives and their family's lives.

Acceptance by schools of the difficulties faced by young carers is needed to ensure that they are not educationally disadvantaged. Practical arrangements to help with homework schedules, late or erratic attendance and underachievement are all needed.

Personal development

The constraints of caring should not affect their ability to develop freely. R. GRIMSHAW, *CHILDREN OF PARENTS WITH PARKINSON'S DISEASE, NATIONAL CHILDREN'S BUREAU, 1994*

Young carers need to be enabled to have opportunities to be just 'children and young people.' They need to be encouraged and enabled to socialise with their peer groups and require the provision of resources for respite and leisure both on their own and with their family. Their caring responsibilities should not prevent them from leading full lives.

6.3 Comparisons with other projects

The issues and experiences recorded in this report reflect those recorded about young carers in other parts of the country.

Needs expressed by the young carers also reflect 'The rights of children who care' (Aldridge, J., Becker, S. *Children Who Care: Inside the World of Young Carers,* Loughborough University, 1993). (See Table 6.1 on page 60).

This is the first piece of research into young carers conducted in a semi-rural area and the findings at this stage suggest that location does not appear to influence the tasks performed by young carers nor the associated emotional and developmental problems.

This study also included a higher percentage of young carers in a supportive role and looked at the experiences of sibling carers and of older former young carers.

Table 6.1 The rights of children who care

Young carers, as children and as carers have:

- *the right to self determination and choice (to be children, carers or both);*
- *the right to be recognised and treated separately from the care receiver;*
- *the right to be heard, listened to and believed;*
- *the right to privacy and respect;*
- *the right to play, recreation and leisure;*
- *the right to education;*
- *the right to health and social care services specific to their needs;*
- *the right to practical help and support, including respite care;*
- *the right to protection from physical and psychological harm (including the right to protection from injury caused by lifting etc);*
- *the right to be consulted and be fully involved in discussions about decisions which affect their lives and the lives of their families;*
- *the right to information and advice on matters that concern them and their families (including benefits and services, medical information etc);*
- *the right to access to trained individuals and agencies who can deliver information and advice with appropriate expertise, in confidence;*
- *the right to independent and confidential representation and advocacy, including befriending.*
- *the right to a full assessment of their needs, strengths and weaknesses, including full recognition of racial, cultural and religious needs;*
- *the right to appeal and complaints procedures that work;*
- *the right to stop caring.*

RECOMMENDATIONS 7

Although provisions for young carers will affect departmental budgets if agencies work together as proposed in this section, then the financial implications for each can be minimised. The main recommendations involve raising levels of awareness, better utilisation of existing services, as well as the provision of some new resources.

Two underlying principles that need to be remembered when working with a family where a child may be caring are:

Think young carer and *Think multi-agency.*

This chapter is divided into four sections. The first outlines the key principles which need to be considered when planning services to support young carers and their families. The second section is written as a series of guidelines which are intended to act as a basis for discussion amongst service providers and to assist with furthering the development of professional practice within both statutory and voluntary sectors. The third section provides a model for assessing and monitoring the needs of young carers and the final section outlines the Winchester Young Carers Project, which has been established as a direct response to this piece of research.

7.1 Key principles

Young carers and their families need support and resources that will:

● maintain family stability;

● ensure that the child's physical, emotional and educational development are not adversely affected;

● ensure that unacceptable levels of care are not undertaken;

● prevent crisis situations from occurring.

The following general principles should be considered by service providers:

● plan together at county and local level in order to implement a joint strategy and make wider use of existing services;

● raise awareness, at all levels and amongst all agencies, of young carers issues;

● fund an independent agency which young carers feel able to approach for support and to access services;

- actively seek to identify young carers and agree a common referral strategy which will incorporate a standard question to be included on all client forms such as general practitioner's records, care receiver's assessment forms, hospital discharge forms, community nurses and health visitors assessment forms;

- develop current assessment procedures to include young carers' needs, ensuring that they are assessed separately from the care receiver's;

- be prepared to listen and believe the children and young people who care;

- make special provision to assess and address the needs of children whose parents have either a mental health problem, or alcohol or drugs related illness;

- facilitate inter-agency liaison and ensure that adults' teams and children's teams are enabled to work in collaboration;

- ensure ongoing contact and reliable service delivery for both young carers and their families.

7.2 Guidelines for working with young carers

The following guidelines suggest a way forward in developing current practice and resources and are intended for discussion and consultation amongst agencies. They are based on the needs expressed by the children, parents and service providers who contributed to this research and also reflect 'The rights of children who care' (see Table 6.1).

General

Provision for the young carer should include:

- assessment and review procedures;

- access to information, counselling, advocacy and emotional support;

- support to ensure personal development and education is not impeded;

- opportunities for respite and time for leisure;

- extra resources for the care receiver in order to reduce the young carer's responsibilities;

- fuller use of available local resources appropriate to a child's needs, such as YMCA National Centre, youth services, community services and existing counselling services.

Guidelines for a young carers co-ordinator

Funding

Young carers' needs cross all service boundaries and therefore it is the responsibility of all agencies, not just social services, to consider funding support for these children.

Independent management of a young carers co-ordinator

A resource is needed not only to link and access service providers but to address young carers' needs independently from those of the care receiver. Although the involvement of health and social service providers and schools is essential if the needs of young carers are to be met, it would be easier if the young carer could access any support or information required from a central point or 'co-ordinator'. In order to gain children's trust and enable them to seek support in confidence, if required, it is suggested that an independently managed young carers project or co-ordinator may be the appropriate way forward. The advantage of establishing an independent project or co-ordinator is that it would be clear to the children that this resource is just for them. It would not become entangled with or compromised by other services or resources.

Role of young carers co-ordinator

It is suggested that a co-ordinator would have overall responsibility for raising awareness and developing professional practice and would:

- act as a focal point for young carers and all agencies and service providers involved with them;

- raise management awareness of the need for inter-agency planning and provision of services, and promote multi-disciplinary co-operation;

- develop awareness-raising programmes on young carers' issues including training and awareness in schools;

- assist with developing a policy for identification, referral and assessment;

- assist with planning and implementing support;

- ensure contact with identified young carers is maintained;

- enable the viewpoint of young carers to be heard and involve young carers in the development of resources and a support group;

- identify ongoing needs for additional resources to support young carers;

- ensure young carers have access to confidential representation, advocacy and a complaints procedure, if required.

Guidelines for schools

Ongoing support at school will lower the stress often surrounding the curriculum, examinations, homework and relationships. Increased awareness in schools about the role of young carers will also help staff and pupils understand the pressures these young people have and how they can help by offering support and encouragement. J. ALDRIDGE, S. BECKER, C. DEARDEN, *PARTNERS IN CARING*, CARERS NATIONAL ASSOCIATION, 1944

In line with working together with other agencies, schools have a duty to establish links within the local community, as well as addressing the overall needs of their pupils. Schools are in daily contact with young carers and should be enabled to recognise a young carer who may require support. A development plan could include:

● consideration by governing bodies of what provision they will make for support in their school, both for the children and to raise awareness of this issue amongst staff;

● promotion of positive images of illness and disabilities to encourage understanding amongst staff members and other pupils and reduce embarrassment experienced by young carers;

● discussion in the personal/social skills part of the curriculum about issues surrounding disabilities and caring, which may help to bring such situations more into the open and facilitate their acceptance;

● the offer of access to information or training to enable staff to recognise signs which may indicate a child is caring, and the sensitive and confidential handling of the situation when a young carer is known to the school;

● allowances for a young carer's inability to spend sufficient time on homework and GCSE coursework to be made if appropriate (this may include notifying the examining authority of the circumstances);

● extra provision to help young carers achieve their full potential, including assessment of any special educational needs they may have themselves;

● full use of internal and external support services available eg. education welfare service, child guidance service, social services, youth services and the voluntary sector.

Guidelines for health and social service providers

Health and social service providers may already be in regular contact with a family where a member has a disability or long-term illness. The following guidelines may be of assistance in helping to tailor assessment procedures and service provision to meet the needs of young carers more appropriately.

● General practitioners should be prepared to take a more pro-active approach in identifying young carers and, having identified them, be prepared to refer them to the appropriate agency or liaise with a young carers co-ordinator, if one is established in the area. Whenever consulting a care receiver, general practitioners could ask themselves, 'Who is doing the caring?' and establish a framework in which information on the health of the family as a whole, rather than just the health of the individual is assessed.

● Hospital admission and discharge notes could be amended to include an applicable question to identify possible young carers.

● Likewise, health visitors, community nurses, school doctors, nurses and adult social services teams could also play an active role in the recognition and support of young carers.

● Both health and social services should be prepared to use adult and disability services to tailor provision to the care receiver in order to reduce the caring responsibilities undertaken by the child.

● If appropriate, all members of the family should be involved in discussions about care arrangements for the care receiver.

● When required, a young carer should be offered individual support on an ongoing, structured basis.

● Provision for respite for young carers should be provided in planning documents.

● Both health and social services should work in unison with other appropriate agencies to ensure that the diverse needs of young carers are met.

7.3 Assessing and monitoring young carers' needs

Assessment guidelines for all agencies

It does not need to be stated that an assessment of a young carer needs to be conducted in a sensitive manner. It can be very painful to discuss all the things your relative cannot do and to talk of the tasks that you perform for them. The children also need to know that their contribution to the family is valued and that they should not feel guilty or threatened by any assessment. It is important to ensure that both family and child feel in control of the situation.

Many children want to care for their relative and, over a period of time, it has become a major part of their life. To suddenly withdraw their right to give care to someone they love could be traumatic.

When assessing young carers' needs, the stability and needs of the whole family, including those of the care receiver, must also be considered. However, the needs of the care receiver should not take precedence over those of the child, particularly if the responsibilities and effects of caring are placing the child 'in need' as defined by the Children Act. Despite this, there will be some cases where non-intervention may be appropriate.

Each assessment will also need to take the family situation into account and address the issue of whether the child's caring responsibilities are at an acceptable or unacceptable level.

A formal assessment could include:

● a checklist of tasks performed by the young carer;

● a checklist of resources already available to the care receiver and the family;

● ascertaining the impact caring responsibilities are having on the young carer's social, personal and educational development and leisure time;

● ascertaining the level of physical/emotional stress;

● clarification of other available resources without raising unrealistic expectations which cannot be met;

● contributions from other agencies involved with the family, if appropriate;

● separate indication of the needs which are specific to the young carers themselves and any support which may be needed for the care receiver in order to reduce the child's caring responsibilities (while considering the needs of the family as a whole).

Regular reviews should be conducted in order to monitor changing needs.

Checklist of possible indicators which may show if a child is caring

This list is intended to highlight indicators which may, individually or together, signify that a child is a young carer.

● Are there any children in the family where the care receiver lives?

● Is there an adult carer responsible for the care receiver in the family home?

● Who looks after the care receiver when the able adult is away from the house (working, shopping or having a break)?

● Does the parent place his/her needs above those of the child?

● Is the child assuming a parental role towards younger able siblings?

● Does the child show signs of false maturity?

● Is the child at times unwell, tired, stressed or depressed?

● Is the child missing school, underachieving or is his/her performance deteriorating?

● Is the child's own health and welfare satisfactory?

● Does the child find it difficult to socialise with his/her peers?

● Is the child clearly not making use of any available leisure activities?

● Is the child withdrawn or isolated?

● Is the child showing unacceptable patterns of behaviour?

7.4 The Winchester Young Carers Project

Funding for a further three year period has been made available by Hampshire County Council Social Services Department, North and Mid Hampshire Health Commission and The Children's Society.

This has allowed for the appointment of a Young Carers Co-ordinator within the Winchester area who will work within the guidelines of this report.

To continue to build upon the involvement of the voluntary sector, the Co-ordinator is to be managed by the local Children's Society team.

The project will have two major areas to concentrate upon. Firstly it will provide direct support facilities for young carers in the Winchester area. The establishment of group and individual support will build on the work already established. Of crucial importance will be the production of a leaflet for other young carers to make the support facilities more widely known. Secondly, it will use this research as a tool to inform the major statutory and voluntary agencies about the varied and extensive needs of young carers. The Co-ordinator will be working to address the awareness levels of the major agencies so that young carers do not remain a hidden group.

The project will retain close links with the carers advisory posts within social services and the other young carers groups developing throughout the county of Hampshire.

The challenge for the future lies not only in the direct support services afforded to young carers, but also in ensuring that their needs are reflected in service planning and resource allocation. Building upon the established links that exist between the providers of services to adults and to children will give a sense of new-found urgency in addressing the needs of young carers in Winchester.

Appendix 1

National and local resources

National resources

ASC (Advice, Advocacy and Representation Service for Children and Young People)

Freephone 0800 616101. This is a confidential service for children and young people which can provide an advocate to help get their wishes heard by the right people. Operated by telephone counsellors.

Benefits

For general information on caring and benefits leaflet FB31, which can be obtained from benefit agencies, gives details on what is available. Freephone 0800 666555 gives advice on social security and freephone 0800 882200 gives advice to people with disabilities and their carers.

Carers National Association

This is a national organisation which supports and campaigns on behalf of carers. The work carried out consists of co-ordinating research, initiating policy, and development and support work nationally. CNA also produces a young carers information pack aimed at young people aged 12–18 who have caring responsibilities, and a young carers newsletter. Information for professionals including recent legislation is also available.

For further information contact: Sylvia Heal, National Young Carers Officer, Carers National Association, 20–25 Glasshouse Yard, London EC1A 4JS. Tel. 0171-490 8818.

Childline

Freephone 0800 1111, Freepost 1111, London, N1 0Q5. This is a free 24-hour national telephone helpline for children and young people in trouble or danger. It offers confidential counselling to any child or young person with any problem.

Local resources

Carers Helpline

Tel. 0345 221122. Available Monday to Friday from 5.00pm to 8.30 am, Saturday, Sunday and Bank Holidays 24 hours. Calls can be made in confidence, no names need be given. The helpline offers a listening ear, information, advice and sources of practical help.

Hampshire Carers Support Team
Tel. 01962 847266 or 847186. The role of the team is to develop support for carers throughout the county. The team produce a carers information folder and a quarterly newsletter. It can also provide a Carers Emergency Card which can be carried by the carer.

Hampshire County Council Social Services Department
Winchester Area Office, tel. 01962 869313

Hantsnet
Hantsnet is a computer network which links local authority departments with one another. It enables swift exchange and dissemination of information.

Help for Health
Freephone 0800 665544. Available from 9.30am to 5pm. Provides details of self-help and support groups, NHS services, medical conditions and treatments.

Pinpoint Directory
Tel. 01703 229017. Provides local information for people with special needs throughout Hampshire.

Winchester Carers Centre
Tel. 01962 842034. Provides a central point for information, advice and support for carers in the community.

Exchange of information

WDCCS (Winchester District Council of Community Service)
Tel. 01962 842293. Provides practical support to voluntary organisations and community groups. It also produces a comprehensive directory of local organisations.

Counselling and advocacy

Face to Face
Tel. 01962 878300. 9a Parchment Street, Winchester. Offers free counselling, information and advice for young people.

Winchester Advocacy Project, WDCCS
Tel. 01962 842293. A new project offering an independent advocacy service for all age groups and needs.

Winchester Child Guidance
Tel. 01962 855477. Can provide help and advice on relationships and emotional wellbeing.

Appendix 2

Legislation which can be used to support the young carer

The Children Act 1989

It is important to remember that the Children Act is addressed to the local authority as a whole and other agencies, not just to the social services department.

The Children Act, Sect 17 (paras 1,10) defines a clear duty to put help into a family where a young person is deemed to be in need and to keep the family together in so doing.

Where a young person's health or development are impaired as a result of their caring responsibilities then they may be 'a child in need' within the terms of the act.

It shall be the duty of every local authority (a) to safeguard and promote the welfare of children within their area who are in need; and (b) so far as is consistent with that duty, to promote the upbringing of such children by their families, by providing a range and level of services appropriate to those children's needs. Sect 17 [1]

A child shall be taken to be in need if (a) he is unlikely to achieve or maintain, or have the opportunity of achieving or maintaining, a reasonable standard of health or development without the provision for him of services by a local authority, or (b) his health or development is likely to be significantly or further impaired, without the provision for him of such services. Sect 17 [10]

Further clarification is given in Volume Two of the Guidance and Regulations.

In assessing individual need, authorities must assess the existing strengths and skills of the families concerned and help them overcome identified difficulties and enhance strengths. Sometimes the needs will be found to be intrinsic to the child; at other times however it may be that parenting skills and resources are depleted or underdeveloped and thus threaten the child's well-being... It may be that the provision of the services to the parent, either under adult disabled persons legislation or under 17(3) of the Act, may safeguard the welfare of children sufficiently to enable the parent to continue looking after him at home. In other cases social problems, unemployment or bereavement, for example, may temporarily reduce the quality of care of children in the family.

1990 NHS & Community Care Act

The great change, effected by this act, was the promotion of needs-led assessment supported by a wider range of flexible health and social services provision to enable clients to be cared for within their own homes, rather than entering institutional care. Such a major change in the provision of services is having an impact on anyone who cares for a relative in their own home, including young carers. There is no specific reference to young carers in this act but these general guidelines are appropriate for the needs of this group of young people.

The NHS & Community Care Guidelines state that the *needs of the carer should be separately assessed... include all carers in decision-making processes* and *ensure that all service providers make practical support for carers a high priority.*

A number of other pieces of legislation or policy commitments, as detailed below, can also be seen to be useful in supporting the needs of young carers.

Social Services Inspectorate

The Social Services Inspectorate is working alongside voluntary organisations and local authorities to continue to develop understanding of how best to meet the needs of young carers. A recent statement to all directors of social services states that *it is essential that the community care assessment focuses on the family and considers how to support the parent and recognise the needs of any young carers.*

Education Act 1993 The Special Educational Needs Code of Practice

This includes the following two clauses which state that there must be:

ongoing provision meeting a wide range of special needs.

partnership between parents and all agencies involved.

Health of the Nation

One of the stated priorities in the Health of the Nation document is to *ensure high quality health and social care in the community in partnership with local authorities.*

United Nations Convention on the Rights of the Child

The UK Government has signed the UN Convention on the Rights of the Child in which several articles are applicable to the rights of children as carers, primarily:

Article 3.1 states that *in all actions concerning children, whether undertaken by public or private social welfare institutions, courts of law, administrative authorities or legislative bodies, the best interests of the child shall be of primary consideration.*

Other articles of the UN Convention which are particularly applicable to the issues surrounding young carers are as follows:

Article 12.1 states *parties shall assure to the child who is capable of forming his or her own views the right to express those views freely in all matters affecting the child, the views of the child being given due weight in accordance with the age and maturity of the child.*

Article 26 states *parties shall recognise for every child the right to benefit from social insurance and shall take the necessary measures to achieve the full realisation of this right in accordance with their national law.*

Article 31.1 states *parties recognise the right of every child to rest and leisure, to engage in play and recreational activities appropriate to the age of the child and to participate freely in cultural life and the arts.*

Article 36 states *parties shall protect the child against all other forms of exploitation prejudicial to any aspects of the child's welfare.*

Appendix 3

Policy guidelines applicable to HCCSSD, Winchester area

Community Care Plan 1994/5
(Hampshire County Council Social Services Department)
This plan does not specifically mention young carers but does include detailed policy statements for both users and carers.

The policy states that the department will ensure that:

- carers needs are separately assessed;

- they have access to information;

- their voice is heard in the consultation process;

- a range of services exists to meet the different needs of individuals and their carers;

- services are flexible and responsive.

Think Carer
(Hampshire County Council 1992)
A policy guide drawn up by a group of carers together with health and social care professionals in the Wessex Health District, to help health and social services respond to the NHS & Community Care Act. 'Think Carer' recognised that a carer can be:

a son or daughter and can be as young as 6 years.

It advocates that:

all health and social services provision should 'think carer' in that part of their assessment of need should include provision for identifying carers.

and that carers are entitled to services which:

- recognise their contribution to care and respect their needs;

- actively involve them in planning and monitoring;

- offer real choice;

- are responsive to individual needs and situations;

- are accessible.

Children First
(Hampshire County Council Social Services Department 1993) A Policy strategy for services for children and families
This has the following statement of principles:

● that in all dealings with a child and his or her parents, it is the child's welfare that is of paramount importance;

● that a child should, whenever possible, stay with his or her birth family, and within his or her own community;

● that children should be protected from neglect, abuse and exploitation.

Hampshire County Council – The Children Act – Policies and Procedures 1991
This includes in its criteria of children in need:

children with caring responsibilities.

Hampshire County Council Policy Statement on Children with Special Needs, 1995
This states that it will implement the Special Needs Code of Practice contained in the 1993 Education Act and advocates two basic principles to ensure that:

● all children are valued, regardless of their abilities and behaviours;

● all children are entitled to have access to a broad, balanced and relevant curriculum which is differentiated to meet individual needs.

Objective 9 states that it will:

in liaison with the Health Commissions and the Social Services Department, establish effective mechanisms for identifying and meeting all the needs of children with severe challenging behaviour and exceptional needs.

One of the requirements of the Special Educational Needs audit is to:

allocate resources to each school on the basis of the assessment of the needs of the children at the school.

Appendix 4

Numbers of household residents with limiting long-term illness in Hampshire by area and age group

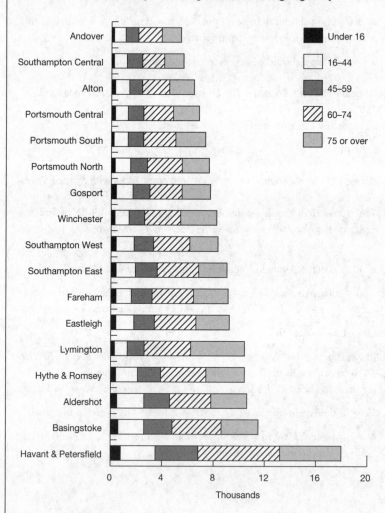

Appendix 5

Hampshire's population in a national context

Total population: 1,595,014
(Source: Hampshire County Council Planning Department)

This appendix provides a small sample of comparitive tables to show Hampshire's population in relation to three other spatial units:
Group A Authorities
The Shire Authorities
England and Wales

Group A Authorities are a group of 18 local authorities which are broadly similar to Hampshire across a range of socio-economic and demographic characteristics. They are:

Avon, Bedfordshire, Berkshire, Buckinghamshire, Cambridgeshire, Cheshire, Essex, Goucestershire, Hampshire, Hereford & Worcester, Hertfordshire, Kent, Leicestershire, Northamptonshire, Oxfordshire, Surrey, Warwickshire and Wiltshire.

The 39 Shire Authorities, including figures for total population,are:

	Total Population
Avon	975,500
Bedfordshire	545,200
Berkshire	769,900
Buckinghamshire	653,660
Cambridgeshire	690,000
Cheshire	983,700
Cleveland	557,000
Cornwall and the Isles of Scilly	478,600
Cumbria	490,193
Derbyshire	953,000
Devon	1,056,900
Dorset	681,800
Durham	594,100
East Sussex	727,600
Essex	1,570,000
Gloucestershire	539,646
Hampshire	1,593,500

Hereford & Worcester	698,300
Hertfordshire	1,006,100
Humberside	881,423
Isle of Wight	130,000
Kent	1,560,000
Lancashire	1,420,600
Leicestershire	910,800
Lincolnshire	608,600
Norfolk	774,200
Northamptonshire	610,000
Northumberland	308,900
North Yorkshire	731,100
Nottinghamshire	1,029,000
Oxfordshire	596,500
Shropshire	421,744
Somerset	478,500
Staffordshire	1,051,800
Suffolk	659,800
Surrey	1,036,700
Warwickshire	494,000
West Sussex	720,770
Wiltshire	585,000

	Hampshire	Group A Authorities	Shire Counties	England and Wales
Percentage of residents				
aged between 0 and 4	6.7	6.6	6.5	6.6
aged between 5 and 9	6.2	6.3	6.2	6.3
aged between 16 and 17	2.6	2.6	2.6	2.5
aged between 18 and 29	18.4	17.9	17.3	18.2
aged between 30 and 44	21.8	22.0	21.3	21.2
aged between 45 and 59/64	19.2	19.5	19.6	19.2
aged 18-59/64	59.4	59.4	58.2	58.6
aged 60/65 or over	18.0	17.9	19.4	18.8
aged 75 or over	6.9	6.7	7.4	7.1
aged 85 or over	3.7	1.5	1.6	1.5
Total resident population	100.0	100.0	100.0	100.0

	Hampshire	Group A Authorities	Shire Counties	England and Wales
Percentage of residents				
% with limiting long-term illness	9.9	10.0	12.8	12.1
% living in private households	98.1	98.5	98.3	98.5
% living in communal establishments	1.9	1.5	1.7	1.5
Percentage of households with:				
child(ren) aged under 5	13.0	12.3	12.5	12.8
2 or more children aged under 16	16.7	16.8	16.1	10.4
only 1 person aged 16 or over with child(ren) aged 0–15	3.0	2.9	3.1	3.7
Percentage of residents who are:				
White	98.1	96.3	97.7	94.1
Black Caribbean	0.2	0.5	0.2	1.0
Black African	0.1	0.1	0.1	0.4
Black Other	0.2	0.2	0.2	0.4
Indian	0.5	1.4	0.6	1.7
Pakistani	0.1	0.5	0.4	0.9
Bangladeshi	0.1	0.1	0.1	0.3
Chinese	0.2	0.2	0.2	0.3
Other - Asian	0.2	0.3	0.2	0.4
Other - Other	0.3	0.4	0.3	0.6
Total	100.0	100.0	100.0	100.0

Appendix 6

ASPECTS OF CARING

Responsibility may be as sole, supportive or sibling carer

Practical and physical tasks may include:

- budgeting
- shopping
- collecting prescriptions and benefits
- housework
- personal care
- dressing
- bathing
- toileting needs
- giving medication
- lifting
- ensuring safety
- communicating for parent
- parenting younger siblings

Emotional issues may include anxiety about:

- care receiver's health
- able parent's wellbeing
- the future
- hereditary factors
- being 'different'

The effects of caring may have a long-term impact on the child's life.

PERSONAL DEVELOPMENT

General

This may include:

- loss of childhood
- false maturity
- behavioural difficulties
- a more caring approach

Family may experience:

- transfer of role
- dysfunction
- closed family environment

There may also be:

- loss of parental authority
- limited family outings
- financial problems

Social life

This may be constrained by:

- caring responsibilities
- finances
- imposed or self-imposed curfew

Young carers may:

- have limited opportunity for making or contacting friends
- have difficulty in relating to peers and in forming relationships
- be withdrawn, isolated, stigmatised or ostracised within their peer group

Psychological and emotional factors

Young carers may feel:

- emotional anxiety
- resentment at demands made
- obligation to care
- guilt/self blame
- depression
- embarrassment
- anger
  fear of:
- the future
- being taken for granted
- failure resulting in parent being received into residential care

Young carers may show unacceptable patterns of behaviour.

— The issues

EDUCATIONAL ISSUES

Young carers may be hidden from schools because school can provide:

- an escape
- stability
- the chance to be like everyone else

Teachers need to:

- be aware of sensitivity of situation
- respect confidentiality

Young carers may:

- be late
- be tired
- miss school
- underachieve
- have difficulty completing homework
- have special needs
- have behavioural difficulties
- need extra time to complete homework tasks and GCSE coursework
- need help to socialise within peer group

NEEDS

Young carers have needs which:

- are complex
- differ with each family situation
- need a multi-agency approach
- can have long-term effects
- need to be recognised by their family

Young carers need to be:

- actively identified
- assessed separately from care receiver
- heard and believed
- approached sensitively and confidentially
- offered support to maintain family stability

offered protection from:

- unacceptable levels of care
- physical harm caused by
  - lifting
  - fatigue
- psychological harm caused by
  - stress
  - dysfunction
  - lost childhood
  - constraints on personal development

offered access to:

- information about
  - parent's illness
  - changes in routine
  - support available
- respite
- advocacy
- counselling
- emotional support

Appendix 7

The reference group

A multi-agency reference group met regularly to support and guide the research. It included the following representatives:

- Pauline Owen, Service Manager for Children and Families
Hampshire County Council Social Services Department, Winchester District

- Mike Winterson, Team Manager for Adult Disabilities and Mental Health
Hampshire County Council Social Services Department, Winchester District

- Jim McGilvery, Divisional Education Welfare Officer (Central Division Education Office)
Hampshire County Council

- Geoff Woollan, Advisor for Carers' Development
Hampshire County Council Social Services Department

- Jan Bartlett, Manager - Health Visiting Services
Elaine Shrine, Health Visitor Representative
Rural District

- Jeremy Coombe, Project Leader
Jill Guppy, Community Development Worker
The Children's Society Community Development Team of Winchester Diocese

Bibliography

Aldridge, J., Becker, S. (1993) *Children Who Care: Inside the World of Young Carers.* Loughborough University Department of Social Sciences.

Aldridge, J., Becker, S.(1994) *My Child, My Carer: The Parents' Perspective.* Loughborough University Department of Social Sciences.

Aldridge, J., Becker, S., Dearden, C. (1994) *Partners in Caring.* Carers National Association and Crossroads UK.

Atkinson, N., Crawforth, M. (1995) *All in the Family: Siblings and Disability.* NCH – Action for Children.

Becker, S. (Editor). (1995) *Young Carers in Europe: An Explanatory Cross-National Study in Britain, France, Sweden and Germany.* Young Carers Research Group and Loughborough University.

Bilsborrow, S. (1992) *You Grow Up Fast As Well: Young carers on Merseyside.* Carers National Association, Personal Social Services and Barnardos.★

Brown, E.M. (1989) *My Parent's Keeper.* Harbinger Press.★

Burnfield, A. (1985) *Multiple Sclerosis: A Personal Exploration.* Souvenir Press.

The Children's Society. *Children Now: A review of 1991.* The Children's Society, Unicef UK and the National Children's Bureau.

Craig, G. (1991) *Cash or Care.* Social Policy Research Unit.

Elliot, A. (1992) *Hidden Children: A Study of Ex Young Carers of Parents with Mental Health Problems in Leeds.* Leeds City Council Department of Social Services.

Ford, J.K., Merriman, P. (1990) *The Gentle Art of Listening: Counselling Skills for Volunteers.* Bedford Square Press.

Gardner, R. (1992) *Supporting Families: Preventative Social Work in Practice.* National Children's Bureau.

Grimshaw, R. (1991) *Children of Parents with Parkinson's Disease: A Research Report for the Parkinson's Disease Society.* National Children's Bureau.★

Johnston, C. (1994) 'Health Care and Social Care Boundaries.' *Nursing Times,* June 29, vol. 90, no. 26.★

Kings Fund Centre. (1988) *Action for Carers: A Guide to Multi-Disciplinary Support at Local Level.*★

Leach, P. (Editor). (1992) *Young Children Under Stress: Practical Guides for Early Years Workers.* Voluntary Organisations Liaison Council for Under Fives.★

Meredith, H. (1991) 'Young Carers'. *Contact,* Summer.

Meredith, H. (1992) 'Supporting the Young Carer'. *Community Outlook,* May.

Mahon, A., Higgins, J. (1995) *Young Carers: An Evaluation of Three Regional Health Authority Funded Projects in Merseyside.*

Marshall, C., Rossman, G. (1989) *Designing Qualitative Research.* Sage.

National Local Authority Forum on Drugs Misuse in conjunction with the Standing Conference on Drug Abuse. (1989) *Drug Using Parents and Their Children.* Forum on Drug Misuse.★

Newell, P. (1991) *The UN Convention and Children's Rights in the UK.* National Children's Bureau.

O'Neill, A. (1988) *The Tameside Research.* Tameside Metropolitan Borough Council.

Stafford, D. (1992) *Children of Alcoholics.* Piatkus.

Twigg, J. (1989) 'Models of Care.' *Journal of Social Policy,* no.18, pages 53-66.★

Tyler, A. (1990) 'Helping the Children to Cope.' *Combat Newsletter,* Spring.

White, P. (1989) 'The Costs of Caring.' *Young People Now,* May.

Voluntary Organisations Personal Social Services Group. (1990) *On Different Tracks: The Inconsistencies Between the Children Act and the Community Care Act.*★

★ Recommended further reading